810.9 Hancock, Carla
H

Seven founders of
American literature

DATE			
JAN 1 7			
JAN 3 1			
1/13/87			
2/24 AM			
2/26 AM			
3/3 AM			
3/7 AM			
12/19/88			
12/20/88			
FEB 2 1 1990			

Seven Founders of American Literature

Seven Founders of American Literature

/ by Carla Hancock

Portrait Drawings by Ted Trinkaus

JOHN F. BLAIR, *Publisher*

/ Winston-Salem, North Carolina

Printed in the United States of America
by HERITAGE PRINTERS, Inc.
Charlotte, North Carolina

LIBRARY OF CONGRESS CATALOGING IN PUBLICATION DATA

Hancock, Carla.
    Seven founders of American literature.

    SUMMARY: Biographies of seven important nine-
teenth century American authors: Cooper, Irving,
Bryant, Poe, Melville, Whitman, and Clemens.
    1. Authors, American—19th century—Biography—
Juvenile literature. [1. Authors, American]
I. Trinkaus, Ted. II. Title.
PS128.H27   810'.9 [B] [920]   75-44173
ISBN 0–910244–87–1

A Word

I wish to express my deep gratitude to Mr. Thomas W. Chandler, Librarian, Oglethorpe University, Atlanta, Georgia, and his staff for their assistance in the research for this book.

CARLA HANCOCK

Contents

The artistic representation of history is a more scientific and serious pursuit than the exact writing of history. For the art of letters goes to the heart of things, whereas the factual report merely collocates details.

ARISTOTLE

Washington Irving

Washington Irving
/ The Man of Many Pen Names

There was great excitement in the city of New York when the newly elected President, George Washington, arrived there in April, 1789. At that time the official presidential residence was in New York City, and all New Yorkers were anxious to get a glimpse of the great man as he moved through the streets.

One of these New Yorkers was six-year-old Washington Irving, named for George Washington. Whenever the President rode by on his horse, Irving's nursemaid would hold her young charge up high above the crowds. Always on the alert for the appearance of the President, the nursemaid spotted him one day entering a shop on Broadway. Quick to seize this unexpected opportunity, she rushed into the store with young Irving. Without excuse or ceremony she approached the President.

"Please, your Excellency," she pleaded in her Scottish accent, "here's a bairn that's called after ye!"

Half a century later, Irving recalled in a letter to a friend that he "laid his hand upon my head, and gave me his blessing." George Washington would have been surprised to know that he had bestowed his blessing upon a future biographer.

Washington Irving was born on April 3, 1783, at 131 William Street in New York, a city still comfortably adorned with remnants of the Dutch architecture that indicated who its original settlers had been.

As a child, Irving was very different from his family and its traditions, though he would always embrace them warmly in his affections. The youngest of eleven children, he was to develop into the family's most talented member. Washington and his father, William Irving, Sr., were of such divergent temperaments that there was little communication between them. But of his mother, Sarah, who "made a point of enriching her husband with at least one child a year, and very often a brace," the author spoke with fondest affection. "I dream of her to this day," he wrote late in his own life, "and wake with tears on my cheeks."

"I was a poor scholar—fond of roguery," Irving confided to a friend. This was the basis of differences between father and son. His father and two brothers, William and Ebenezer, who operated a hardware business, were content to be merchants. The senior Irving, a native of the Orkney Islands off the coast of Scotland, was representative of the sternly persevering mercantile aspect of old New York; Washington, his youngest son, bore witness to the city's cultural development and was "apt to see clear through a subject, where the penetration of ordinary people extends but halfway," as he later wrote in Diedrich Knickerbocker's *A History of New York*.

From childhood Irving possessed an exceptional poise and was extremely gentle in nature. Once when he saw one of his schoolmates physically punished he became ill. He was also a dreamy child who thrived on fantasy. In his father's view he was scatterbrained and ineffectual. But although he saw the world through romantic eyes, he was not such a dreamer that he shunned the practical. His ambition, when channeled into a creative project, was boundless. Drawn naturally to books, his reading was limited by the selections in his father's well-stocked but conservative library. His imagination demanded the exciting and adventurous, a need only partly filled by the authors available to him. The works of Chaucer, Spenser, and Shakespeare were among those in the family library, along with the adventures of Robin Hood, Sinbad the Sailor, and Robinson Crusoe. More appealing were the local newspapers, which offered an even wider range of interest for Washington's young and active intellect. They carried the latest works of English and European authors, printed without the authors' permission.

An unobtrusive set of books entitled *The World Displayed* mysteriously found its way into the family library when Washington was about ten years old. They had been placed there, no doubt, by the thoughtful hand of William, Ebenezer, John, or Peter, Washington's older brothers; or maybe by Anne, one of his sisters. These travel sketches delighted Washington's young heart, although his dour Scotsman father would have firmly disapproved of such frivolous books. He was a sedate, conscientious, God-fearing man, who possessed the strict nature of an old Scottish Covenanter. He was unsympathetic toward the amusements of his children. "I was led to think that somehow or other every thing that was pleasant was wicked," Irving was to recall in later years.

However much Mr. Irving may have attemped to instill his gloomy view of life in his children, it evidently had little effect on them. Least of all did it change Washington's naturally buoyant, happy nature. He simply continued to enjoy the little books and even took them to school with him, where he read them during periods set aside for study. One day he was caught reading one of these "forbidden" books in school. His teacher ordered him to remain after class, but the anticipated punishment did not take place. Upon investigation, the teacher, who was more progressive than the boy's father, realized his surreptitious reading was constructive in nature and complimented Washington on the excellent taste he showed in his selection of books.

Irving's formal education was completed before he was sixteen. Unlike his older brothers, he did not go on to Columbia College. Through choice, he continued his education alone and in 1799 entered a law office to prepare for the bar examination.

He did not like the study of law, which he thought of as drudgery. It demanded "a fervent zeal for the correct administration of justice and a disinterested devotion" he did not possess. But he had to have a career, and law, the most profitable and socially respected profession at this period in American history, offered the least objectionable course. Lawyers were still in demand to assist in the unraveling of the ownership disputes which followed the American Revolution and continued well into the nineteenth century. Washington's older brother, John Treat Irving, was a lawyer and became the First Judge of the Court of Common Pleas.

While Irving was reading law in the office of Josiah Hoffman, he was given time off to make a trip up the Hudson River to visit two older sisters in Albany, New York. Though he did not know it then, he was to become the first American author to describe "the Kaatskill mountains . . . a dismembered branch of the great Appalachian family . . . seen away to the west of the river, swelling up to a noble height, and lording it over the surrounding country."

The departure of the sloop on which his passage was to be made was delayed for several days. Her hold had to be loaded with freight and her cabins filled with passengers to make the trip profitable to her owners. Irving wrote:

"Days were consumed in 'drumming up' a cargo. This was a tormenting delay to me who was about to make my first voyage, and who, boy-like, had packed up my trunk on the first mention of the expedition. How often that trunk had to be unpacked and repacked before we sailed!"

This was Irving's first contact with the wild beauty of the Hudson River scenery, and his journal, which he kept during the voyage, is a clear reflection of the creative influence the great river and its accumulated traditions were to have on him.

"But of all the scenery of the Hudson," he later recorded, "the Kaatskill Mountains had the most witching effect on my boyish imagination. Never shall I forget the effect upon me of the first view of them predominating over a wide extent of country, part wild, woody, and rugged; part softened away into all the graces of cultivation. As we slowly floated along, I lay on the deck and watched them through a long summer's day; undergoing a thousand mutations under the magical effects of atmosphere; sometimes seeming to approach; at other times to recede; now almost melting into hazy distance, now burnished by the setting sun, until, in the evening, they printed themselves against the glowing sky in the deep purple of an Italian landscape."

The deep impressions of this magnificent country were to flow forth in Irving's prose of later years. "The whole neighborhood abounds with local tales, haunted spots, and twilight superstitions," he recorded in "The Legend of Sleepy Hollow." "Stars shoot and meteors glare oftener across the valley than in any other part of the country, and the nightmare . . . seems to make it the favorite scene of her gambols. The dominant spirit . . . that haunts this enchanted region . . . is the apparition of a figure on horseback without a head."

In 1803, while Irving was still studying law, he was invited on an expedition that Josiah Hoffman, with whom he was studying, formed for an exploratory trip to Canada. Hoffman had purchased a large tract of land there and planned to develop it. Irving kept a journal of the trip. Although the pages were written in haste, this journal is a graphic record of the difficult conditions under which people then traveled. At the close of one day's journey, Irving wrote: "In several parts of the road I had been up to my middle in mud and water, and it was equally bad, if not worse, to attempt to walk in the woods on either side." Travel was not for the faint of heart.

At one point during their tour of eastern Canada, the party spent the night in a lodge constructed of logs. A French woman operated it, and both she and her lodge were filthy. Nothing was more disgusting to Irving than dirt. Before he left the next morning he could not resist the impulse to write these lines over the fireplace:

> Here Sovereign Dirt erects her sable throne,
> The house, the host, the hostess all her own.

Several years later, Mr. Hoffman made another expedition into Canada, this time accompanied by Judge William Cooper, father of the novelist James Fenimore Cooper. Hoffman drew Judge Cooper's attention to the lines inscribed by Irving. The Judge, who had lived for many years in the wilderness of central New York State, knew the scarcity of refinements on the frontier of any civilization. He added this sage advice under Irving's lines:

> Learn hence, young man, and teach it to your sons,
> The wisest way's to take it as it comes.

Resuming their journey, Irving and his friends were soon stranded in a storm on what seemed to be a disappearing road. They found a one-room hut in the wilderness, where they spent the night. But they were not alone; they shared the hut with fifteen other people, two of whom were ox-team drivers, one of them "the most impudent, chattering, forward scoundrel" Irving had ever known.

"I never passed so dreary a night in my life," Irving wrote in his journal. "The rain poured down incessantly, and I was frequently obliged to hold up an umbrella to prevent its beating through the roof on the ladies as they slept. I was awake almost all night, and several times heard the crash of the falling trees, and . . . the long dreary howl of a wolf."

The party resumed its journey the next morning, encountering further hardships, adventures, misadventures—and Indians. At one Indian camp, where they were welcomed with great ceremony, Hoffman, in a spirit of jovial fun, asked the Indians to give Irving an Indian name, to which they readily agreed. With great dignity one of the Indian chiefs took Irving's hand and escorted him to the center of the compound. The chief then began a slow dance around Irving, to the accompaniment of a low chant. The other Indians formed a circle around the two and now and then contributed a confirming "Ugh, ugh." The dance stopped as abruptly as it had begun, and the chief made a speech, incomprehensible to Irving. Then Irving received his new name, *Vomente*, which means "good to everybody."

But Irving was to have his playful revenge upon Hoffman. He told the Indians that they had conferred an honor upon an unworthy object—the really important member of the party was Mr. Hoffman. The Indians insisted that another name-giving ceremony be performed. To Irving's great delight, Hoffman had to go through the same rites, receiving the name *Citrovani*, or "Shining Man."

"I was always fond of visiting new scenes, and observing strange characters and manners," Irving was to write in his *Sketch-Book*. "How wistfully would I wander about the pier heads in fine weather, and watch the parting ships, bound to distant climes—with what longing eyes would I gaze after their lessening sails, and waft myself in imagination to the ends of the earth!"

Irving's dream was to be realized in his twenty-first year. He was in poor health, and after a conference with the concerned family, his oldest brother William decided that Washington should be sent abroad. Despite his travel hunger, his leave-taking proved difficult. As he wrote a friend from Bordeaux: "I felt heavy-hearted on leaving the city, but the severest moments of my departure were when I lost sight of the boat in which were my brothers . . . and when the steeples of the city faded from my view. It seemed as if I had left the world behind me, and was cast among strangers . . . sick and solitary." To William he wrote, reassuringly: "My health is much better than when I left New York." In a postscript he added: "Bonaparte is declared

Emperor of the Gauls . . . ." Irving had arrived in France at a most critical period, and this was to cause him some inconvenience. He was suspected of being a British spy, and his passport was withheld until he could prove otherwise.

As he traveled by sea from Genoa to Messina, Italy, Irving's ship was stopped by a privateer's ship, "about the size of one of our Staten Island ferryboats," he wrote. "A more villainous-looking crew I never beheld. Their dark complexions, rough beards, and fierce black eyes scowling under enormous bushy eyebrows, gave a character of the greatest ferocity to their countenances. They were . . . armed with cutlasses, stilettoes, and pistols." There was certainly a sinister atmosphere to the affair. But after ransacking the American ship, the privateers found Irving's letters of introduction to the Governor of Malta and released the vessel.

Just as Irving's ship arrived at the Messina Straights, Nelson's fleet entered in pursuit of the French fleet. That morning "two ships-of-the-line were seen entering the Straits," he reported. "Several more ships made their appearance, and it was ascertained to be the English fleet. In a short time Lord Nelson's ship, the Victory, hove in sight. They all advanced most majestically up the straits. . . . We . . . wished to have a good view of them. . . . [The fleet] consisted of eleven sail-of-the-line, three frigates, and two brigs, all in prime order, and most noble vessels. . . . They continued in sight all day. It was very pleasing to observe with what promptness and dexterity the signals were made, answered, and obeyed. It seemed as a body of men under perfect discipline. Every ship appeared to know its station immediately, and to change position agreeably to command, with the utmost precision. Nelson has brought them to perfect discipline . . . ."

Irving thought of the gallant fleet at Messina when, some months later, during the performance of a play he was attending in London, an actor appeared on the stage to make the electrifying announcement that Trafalgar was won and Nelson dead.

When Irving returned from Europe in 1806 he was in good

health and excellent spirits; his mind was broadened and his manners polished. After the charm and intrigue of the Old World, the Hoffman law firm held even less appeal for him than before his trip abroad. Law, as a profession, seemed to the young gallant flat and dull, totally without inspiration.

But not long after his return from Europe Irving came to the startling realization that he was in love with Matilda Hoffman, youngest daughter of Josiah Hoffman. He had been charmed by her ever since she was a little girl but had always thought of her older sister Ann in romantic terms. Matilda was now a young lady of fourteen. Irving, at twenty-two, had been infatuated with many girls before this time. But Matilda was different; he wished to *marry* her.

There was one obstacle: He had no financial security to offer her. Although he was popular as a humorous writer, his pen could not be relied upon to support a wife. Even after six years of study, he still showed little promise in the law and had not passed his bar examination. Mr. Hoffman was aware of the young man's feelings toward his daughter. He was very fond of Irving and considered him a desirable match for Matilda. He offered him a partnership in his law firm with the understanding that he would apply himself diligently to the work.

Though the law was distasteful to him, the thought of some-day marrying Matilda spurred him on to greater efforts. Since the Hoffman law firm was the most prominent in the city, he had everything to gain. For the next three years Irving worked at the study of law. Every free moment was given to the courtship of his beloved Matilda. There were no two happier young people in New York City. Together they enjoyed books, plays, lectures, dances, and quiet walks along the waterfront.

But in February, 1809, Matilda became seriously ill. She had always been frail; her delicacy was part of her appeal to Irving. The illness caused her to decline rapidly. Irving, along with her family, watched helplessly. Matilda died on April 26, 1809, two months after the illness had first appeared.

Irving's hopes, his plans, his dreams, all came to an abrupt halt with Matilda's death. He was too heartsick to continue even a feigned interest in the law. It no longer mattered whether he had any money or not. He was sure of only one thing at that moment: With Matilda gone, he would not need to support a wife. Fifteen years later he would write of her:

"She died in the flower of her youth and of mine but she has lived for me ever since in all woman kind. I see her in their eyes —and it is the remembrance of her that has given a tender interest in my eyes to every thing that bears the name of woman."

Irving never really recovered from the loss of Matilda, although he had many women friends throughout his life. He was a normal man and found existence almost unbearable without feminine companionship. There is evidence that on at least two occasions he considered marriage. One of the young women was Miss Emily Foster, whom he met in Dresden, Germany. Emily, an English girl, was less than half his age. At the time Irving was forty years old and Emily was eighteen. On another occasion, his name was linked with Mary Wollstonecraft Shelley, the widow of the poet Percy Bysshe Shelley. Irving is known to have been romantically involved with a number of other beautiful women. Yet he never married.

Of all these lovely women, only Matilda found her way into his diaries, journals, and other manuscripts—and this long after she was gone.

The loss of Matilda brought a complete change in the direction Irving's life was to take. Since he had permanently turned his back on law as a profession, there was nothing left for him except his pen. As early as 1802, when he was nineteen years old, he had written a series of humorous articles for the *Morning Chronicle*, a daily newspaper edited by his brother, Peter Irving. The first of the articles appeared on November 15, 1802. The series was titled *The Letters of Jonathan Oldstyle, Gent.*, and reflected the frivolous, witty nature of the young writer, who remained anonymous to the public. Aaron Burr, well aware of the writer's identity, found Irving's humor so entertaining that he clipped the articles from the paper and sent them to his daughter Theodosia with the notation that they "would not, perhaps, merit so high an honour as that of being perused by your—eyes and touched by your fair hands, but that [they are] the production of . . . the youngest brother of Dr. Peter Irving . . . ."

Irving had wisely chosen not to sign his own name to the Oldstyle letters, although it became generally known that he was the author of them. It is not difficult to imagine his staid father's disapproval when, in one Oldstyle letter, Washington publicly confessed: "There is no place of public amusement of which I am so fond as the Theatre." Adding insult to the senior Irving's injured feelings, he continued: "I find there is no play, however poor or ridiculous, from which I cannot derive some entertainment." Of the actors in the play under his critical eye, he observed: "They talked for some time, though I could not understand the drift of their discourse, so I amused myself with eating pea-nuts."

Irving's critical pen missed none of the Park Theatre's provincial elements; the actors, the acting, the design and decor of the theatre, its audience—all came under his critical observation. Although he had written the Oldstyle letters when he was only nineteen, he showed a sharp awareness of what the arts lacked in America. Among other points for improvement, he suggested the theatre distribute umbrellas to the audience in the pit to protect them from the candle grease that fell from the grand chandelier.

After his return to New York from Europe, Irving became increasingly the sharp-eyed observer and critic. Little escaped his pen. His keen powers of observation are evident in *Salmagundi; or, the Whim-Whams and Opinions of Launcelot Langstaff, Esq., and Others*, a spoof periodical written and published by the "lads of Kilkenny," an informal group of the young blades of New York, of which Washington and his brothers William,

Ebenezer, and Peter were members. The Irving brothers and James Kirke Paulding, another member of the group and a writer, together wrote *Salmagundi*, published in 1807.

Salmagundi, its bumptious authors explained, strove to "instruct the young, reform the old, correct the town, and castigate the age . . . an arduous task."

During the months before Matilda's death, Irving had been preparing his manuscript, Diedrich Knickerbocker's *A History of New York from the Beginning of the World to the End of the Dutch Dynasty*. He had begun this work with Peter at the happiest time of his life. Now it provided an escape from his grief. Begun as a burlesque on a popular handbook of New York sights and scenes, it was carried out in so subtle a way that everyone in New York City believed it to be authentic. An advertisement was placed in the New York *Evening Post* on October 26, 1809. It informed the reader of the distressing disappearance of "a small elderly gentleman, dressed in an old black coat and cocked hat, by the name of *Knickerbocker*." Eleven days later, on November 6, there was a reply to this advertisement from "A Traveller":

To the Editor of the Evening Post:
SIR,—Having read in your paper of the 26th October last, a paragraph respecting an old gentleman by the name of *Knickerbocker*, who was missing from his lodgings; if it would be any relief to his friends, or furnish them with any clue to discover where he is, you may inform them that a person answering the description given, was seen by the passengers of the Albany stage, early in the morning, about four or five weeks since, resting himself by the side of the road, a little above King's Bridge. He had in his hand a small bundle, tied in a red bandana handkerchief; he appeared to be travelling northward, and was very much fatigued and exhausted.

Seth Handaside, Knickerbocker's landlord, made a public announcement on November 16 stating that he had found "*a very curious kind of a written book*" among the old man's possessions. He further stated that if Knickerbocker did not return immediately to pay what he owed for his room and board the book would be sold to satisfy the debt. On November 28 another notice appeared which announced publication of the book and confirmed that it was being published "to discharge certain debts [the author] has left behind." The title of the book was *A History of New York*. There was no advance hint as to the humorous nature of the book, but "it took with the public and gave me celebrity," Irving rejoiced.

After the United States and England became involved in the War of 1812, the Irving brothers' hardware business began to suffer. As was the case with the majority of New York City merchants, most of the Irvings' stock was imported from England. When the war with England began, many of these imported items were cut off by the blockade of the port of New York. To add to the merchants' problems, Americans refused to buy English goods. The Irving brothers found themselves in a serious condition. What stock they had on hand in New York did not sell, and the warehouses in England were overstocked. Peter Irving managed the Liverpool branch of the business. Since he was unable to ship stock to America, that part of the business was on the verge of bankruptcy.

In a united effort to stave off their mutual financial crisis, a group of New York merchants went in protest to Washington, D.C. The Irving brothers delegated Washington, a silent partner in the firm, to join this group in the nation's capital. Although there was little that these merchants could accomplish, Washington found the stay in the capital very beneficial. While there, he was asked to become the editor of the *Analectic Magazine*, published in Philadelphia. He had always avoided editorial positions, though many had been open to him, but now he accepted the offer and began his editorial duties early in 1813. The magazine failed two years later. Irving's name and pen had helped to increase the subscription list considerably, but poor financial management ruined the publication.

In the meantime, the war with England raged on. Irving had been relatively indifferent to the conflict until August 24, 1814, when the British burned Washington, D.C., to the ground. Irving's patriotic feelings were so stirred by this outrageous act that he joined the New York State Militia a few days later. He was made a colonel and served as aide-de-camp to Governor Daniel Tompkins of New York, who was also Commander of the Militia. By December, 1814, the war was almost over and Irving resigned his post in the militia.

Six months later, on May 25, 1815, Irving sailed for Liverpool, England. The immediate reason for this trip was to help Peter salvage what was left of that branch of the hardware business. But Irving was not to return to America for seventeen years. After a three-year struggle against bankruptcy, Peter and Washington closed the Liverpool office and warehouse. With the income from the business gone, Washington was forced to turn to his pen for support. He had written nothing since the publication of *A History of New York*.

Irving was fortunate to have the home of his sister Sarah and her husband as a retreat in England during this period of financial difficulty and mental depression. One evening he and his brother-in-law recalled some of the Hudson River legends. Suddenly Irving was released from his depression of many months. An idea for a story had come to him, and he rushed to his room to record it on paper.

Once in his room, he could not write fast enough to keep up with the ideas that came. He wrote throughout the night, and when the light of dawn filled his room, he was still at work. It was not until he was called to breakfast that he laid aside his pen. He took his manuscript downstairs with him and read it aloud to the family. The story which he had so rapidly put down on paper during the night was "Rip Van Winkle," the first in a collection of tales to be included in his volume, *The Sketch-Book of Geoffrey Crayon, Gent.*, published 1819–20. Rip lived in an old

Dutch village at the foot of the Kaatskill Mountains, within view of the Hudson River, in the period when "the country was yet a province of Great Britain." He was "a simple good-natured man; he was, moreover, a kind neighbor, and an obedient henpecked husband." Yet Rip was decidedly lazy, and this kept him in constant trouble with his wife. His two favorite occupations were sitting in front of the local inn philosophizing with his cronies and wandering through the mountains with his gun and his dog Wolf. On one of these expeditions he met a strange dwarf of a man who invited him to join him and some similarly strange companions in a drinking party and a game of ninepins in a remote valley. Rip drank too much and fell asleep.

When he woke up, he noticed that his joints were stiff and that his beard had grown a foot long. Returning to his village, he found it changed almost beyond recognition, familiar landmarks gone, his house deserted and in ruin, strangers everywhere. Gradually it was revealed to him that he had slept for twenty years. He was reunited with a married daughter, who took him to live with her. Rip adjusted to his altered world, where, "instead of being a subject of his Majesty George the Third, he was now a free citizen of the United States," who contentedly assumed the role of village patriarch.

Another tale in *The Sketch-Book* is "The Legend of Sleepy Hollow," a humorous account of a superstitious country schoolmaster named Ichabod Crane, his misadventures as an unsuccessful suitor to Katrina Van Tassel, daughter of a wealthy Dutch farmer, and his fateful encounter with the Headless Horseman. The scene for this tale is the Hudson River Valley just above what is now New York City.

The Sketch-Book was first published in the United States in seven installments which began in June, 1819. It was published as a single volume in England in February, 1820. *Bracebridge Hall*, a similar collection of tales, was published in 1822.

Irving's determination to write had a final test. Before *The*

Sketch-Book was published, his brothers William and Ebenezer procured a post for him as First Clerk of the Navy Department, which would lead to the position of Secretary of the Navy. Irving actually had no qualifications for this appointment. His study and practice of law had not been a success, and he had not done very well in managing his father's business affairs in England. The appointment was a political "deal," the result of his brothers' influence in Washington.

If this offer had been presented immediately on the heels of bankruptcy, Irving would have accepted it. But his purpose was established. "My pride was up," he said. "I would receive nothing as a boon granted to a ruined man—I was resolved . . . to raise myself once more by my talents . . . ."

"I am determined not to return home," he wrote Ebenezer, "until I have sent some writings before me that shall . . . make me return to the smiles, rather than skulk back to the pity of my friends." The first bundle of reviews of *The Sketch-Book*, which William sent to him, insured its success. The book also had the distinction of being the first American work of fiction to command widespread respect in England.

Irving had grown weary of the sights, sounds, and smells of England. Germany, where the people "are full of old customs . . . obsolete in other parts of the world," offered a new source of inspiration. With encouragement from Sir Walter Scott, whom he visited at Abbotsford, he departed for Germany. Scott had suggested that Irving write a book on German folklore. With characteristic enthusiasm, Irving totally immersed himself in German life and legend. He was enthralled with the country:

"I feel the value of life and health now in a degree that I never did before. I have always looked upon myself as a useless being, whose existence was of little moment. I now think, if I live and enjoy my health, I may be of some use to those who are most dear to me."

Irving made Dresden his headquarters. He was presented at

the court of Frederick Augustus I and took part in the brilliant court life. He traveled, collected material for *Tales of a Traveller*, studied German, wrote parts for court frolics, visited art galleries, but did no serious writing.

At Salzburg he recorded: "There are little men and women that live in the interior of the mountain, and sometimes visit the Cathedral of Salzburg. There is a hole in the foundation, leading to water, through which it is said they enter. They say the Cathedral was built upon what was once a lake."

Irving scoured Germany for every available scrap of folklore. He searched for gnomes, pixies, and phantom armies from the North Sea to the Austrian border, along the Rhein River, up the Neckar, and down the Danube; he made notes on castles steeped in legend, ancient fortresses, and decayed monasteries. He read deeply in German authors who had plumbed the depths of their national folklore. He crammed his notebooks with tales, legends, and lore from Germany's past, all in preparation for a book he planned to write; a book lost in procrastination, indecisiveness, and fragmentation. After moving on to Paris, where he planned to settle down to consistent work on the book of German mythology, Irving again frittered away his time in idle pursuits.

In 1826, discouraged by the critics' unfriendly reception of *Tales of a Traveller*, Irving went to Spain: "a stern, melancholy country, with rugged mountains, and long sweeping plains, destitute of trees . . . silent and lonesome, partaking of the savage and solitary character of Africa," as he described it in *The Alhambra.*

The mood of Spain was well suited to Irving's feelings of desolation. He thought his career as an author had come to a close, but shortly after he arrived in Spain he was asked to translate a biography of Christopher Columbus from Spanish into English. His brother Peter, who had accompanied him to Spain, agreed to assist in the undertaking. After Irving had worked on the biography for three months, he reached the conclusion that the original text was too chronological to be translated into an interesting English narrative. He decided instead to write an original biography of Columbus from the material at his disposal. By the time he had been at work for six months on *A History of the Life and Voyages of Christopher Columbus*, he had accumulated a corps of translators, advisers, and assistants. He wrote a friend: "I am absolutely fagged and exhausted with hard work. . . . I never worked so hard, nor so constantly for such a length of time; but I was determined not to stop until I had made a rough draft of the whole work." But in a later letter, he added: "I find there is nothing keeps up my spirits more than hard work." This was the turning point in Irving's life: Never again did he indulge his habits of idleness and aimless activity. While his secretaries were preparing the first part of his manuscript for the publisher, he was writing the later chapters. "You have no idea what a laborious and entangling job it is," he wrote. "There are so many points in dispute, and so many of a scientific nature into which I have been obliged to enter with great study and examination."

With assistants to lighten the burden of mechanical details, Irving had time to begin research on and write a rough draft of *The Conquest of Granada* long before he completed his biography of Columbus. To authenticate portions of the material he planned to include in *The Conquest* it was necessary for him to go to Granada, which lay sheltered "in the lap of the Sierra Nevada." His visit to the ancient city, dominated by the towers of the Alhambra, stirred his mind with ideas for another book. The Alhambra, a fortress and palace of the Moors during their occupation of Spain, was still used on occasion by the Governor of Granada. Upon being informed that Irving was working on a book about the fortress, the governor made the Alhambra's royal apartment available for the author's use.

"I am so in love with this apartment," Irving wrote, "that I can hardly force myself from it to take my promenades. I sit by my window until late at night, enjoying the moonlight and listening to the sound of the fountains and the singing of the nightingales."

Isolated within the walls of the Alhambra from American and British society, Irving heard nothing but the Spanish tongue for almost four months. Except for the caretaker, Doña Antonia Molina and her family, the Alhambra was inhabited only by beggars and other derelicts.

Irving had hardly begun work on his book when a letter arrived offering him another political appointment: Secretary of the American Legation in London. The only qualifications he had for this appointment were that through his books, particularly *The Sketch-Book*, he had gained wide appeal as an author in England, and that he had lived there on two occasions. When the Republic of the United States of America was young, it was the practice to send a man abroad in a diplomatic post who was personally well known. At a later date, Irving's knowledge of Spain and her people would win him the post of Minister to Spain. As time and experience would prove, his understanding of Spain was his most valuable asset as a diplomat.

Irving was not anxious to accept the appointment to the American Legation in London. He later wrote a friend:

"As it appeared to be the general wish of my friends that I should accept this appointment I have done so; but I assure you when I took my last look at the Alhambra from the mountain road of Granada, I felt like a sailor who has just left a tranquil port to launch upon a stormy and treacherous sea."

Although Irving did not feel that he possessed a natural skill for diplomacy, the flexibility of his personality fitted him perfectly for the position. He at first underrated his natural capacity for the post, as well as for the duties it involved. He had planned to complete *The Alhambra* manuscript after arriving in London, but the demands on his time were too great. The Ambassador became ill, and Irving was made acting chargé d'affairs. Severe trials nagged at the legation, the most important being the mutual distrust between England and America. Irving was virtual head of the legation from June 22, 1831, to April 1, 1832, when the new ambassador arrived from America and Irving left for home. He had been gone seventeen years.

New York welcomed him with a public dinner at the City Hotel, an ordeal he contemplated with horror because he knew he would be called upon to make a speech. But at least it gave him an opportunity to vindicate his patriotism against those who criticized him for staying abroad too long: "I am asked how long I mean to remain here? They know but little of my heart or my feelings who can ask me this question. I answer, as long as I live." His words brought shouts, cheers, bravos, and the waving of handkerchiefs.

Irving had stayed abroad because it was much cheaper to live in Europe than in America. Many nineteenth-century American authors lived abroad for this reason. At first Irving's share from the family hardware business was enough to support him in Europe. Later, after the business failed, the royalties he was beginning to receive from his books provided his support.

The Alhambra was published in 1832, after Irving's return to America. It held such a strong appeal for readers that there was clamor for a book from him on a native subject. To familiarize himself with his own country he made a broad tour of the South and West, where he found his name and books well known and read, even in the smallest river towns.

Just as Walt Whitman was to recognize the unlimited potential of the western frontier, Irving saw in the West a promise beyond anything yet dreamed of by Americans. Although his glimpses of this promise are reflected in *A Tour on the Prairies* (1835), *Astoria* (1836), and *The Adventures of Captain Bonneville* (1837), he did not have the affinity with this new aspect of American life to translate freely what he saw and felt. Irving's forte was in the ancient: the myth and legend of what had gone before, not in what was to come.

After Irving returned to America, his first undertaking was to find a home. When he left for Europe in 1815, he had been living away from his parents' home for several years, but he had never actually established a home of his own. Like many young bachelors, he had found boardinghouses more suitable to his needs. Not only did he now need to make a home for himself and his brother Peter, who had never married, but also for his brother Ebenezer, who was in need of more suitable living quarters. Ebenezer was now alone with his five daughters and had serious financial problems. Irving was eventually to shoulder the entire support of these girls.

It was more than agreeable to all concerned that Irving should provide a home large enough to accommodate them all. Irving found an old Dutch cottage on the bank of the Hudson River, two miles south of Tarrytown, New York. He had it developed into a comfortable home by the addition of numerous rooms and architectural features which reflected the many years he had lived abroad. Irving named the rambling cottage "Sunnyside," suggesting the satisfying way of life which was to develop there. Although Irving had many financial struggles during the remainder of his life, the love and gentle affection showered upon him by his nieces made up for his problems. There was never a dull moment at Sunnyside, because it was the center of much activity. Along with Irving's industrious literary labors, there was a steady stream of visitors, including other members of his family, literary friends and figures who sought him out, political dignitaries from Washington, D.C., and visitors from Europe.

As the years passed, Irving became more and more involved in American life. He had lived abroad for so long that he felt a stranger to his native soil. His longing for Europe, particularly Spain, lessened as home ties increased. In 1834, *The Southern Literary Messenger* selected him as one of the five most distinguished authors in the country, and by 1837, when his prowess as an author is considered to have reached its peak, he was acknowledged to be America's leading writer.

Irving also became a leader in civic and political activities, a bank director, and counselor on European and Spanish affairs. In 1840 he turned Whig, to support President Harrison, who died a month after taking office. Harrison was succeeded by Tyler. Through the efforts of the Whig leader Daniel Webster, an admirer of Irving, the author was offered the post of Envoy Extraordinary and Minister Plenipotentiary to Spain. Irving hesitated, but two elements combined to influence his decision: the memory of Spain's beauty, and his increasing financial problems. His planned biography of Washington could be written in Madrid as conveniently as in Tarrytown, New York. He accepted the post and sailed for Spain.

After brief stops in London and Paris to assemble his staff, Irving reached Madrid, from which he supervised the consuls at Malaga and Barcelona. His intimate knowledge of Spain's history and his written works about the country were most effective factors in his diplomatic relations there. All his works had been translated into Spanish, and the people were closely acquainted with the author who had praised their country in such magnificent prose. They loved him because he loved Spain.

Upon being informed of Irving's appointment as Minister to Spain, the Spanish Minister to Washington, D.C., said:

"He is one of the men of greatest reputation, as much in America as in Europe, for the purity and elegance with which he writes the English language, and he has a most favorable opinion of our country, our customs and the character of our people."

When Irving arrived in Spain in 1842, the internal politics of the country were in turmoil. There was a struggle going on for the control of Spain. The Regent Espartero, who represented twelve-year-old Princess Isabella, the natural heir to the throne, and his enemy Narváez were fighting, Espartero to hold his position and control of Isabella, and Narváez to overthrow the Espartero government and gain control of the Princess and the government. Because of the chaotic situation, there were constant changes in Spain's parliamentary body. It was extremely difficult for Irving to carry on even basic negotiations with the government. In a dispatch to Washington, D.C., he described his position as being "like bargaining at the window of a railroad car: before you can get a reply to a proposition, the other party is out of sight."

As the new American Minister to Spain, Irving was not even sure to whom he should present his credentials: Princess Isabella or the Regent Espartero. Since the government of the United States saluted the Regent, Irving followed suit.

In spite of his diplomatic acumen, Irving, along with the people of Spain, did not comprehend the motives of the self-seeking Espartero. Irving honored the dictator with a trust he did not deserve and accepted without question the claims that he was the innocent target of attempted assassinations and conspiracies.

Irving was fascinated by the revolution, which broke out into open warfare in June, 1843, almost a year after he took up his duties as Minister to Spain. He found it exciting entertainment; it appealed to his romantic senses as a writer. The color, the drama, the suspense were all there, just waiting for his pen. In a letter he described the situation in Madrid: ". . . all the gates were strongly guarded; the main squares were full of troops, with cannon planted at the entrances of the streets opening into them." In another letter he continued: "Troops were stationed in the houses along the main streets, to fire upon the enemy from the windows and balconies, should they effect an entrance; and it was resolved to dispute the ground street by street, and to make the last stand in the royal palace . . . ."

By day he watched the riots in the streets from his window in the American Embassy. After dark he could not resist moving about the streets of Madrid and working his way to the center of the city to observe the violence and disorder which reigned in every quarter. He watched at the gates of the city where the sound of the cannon drowned out every other sound.

According to rumor, Narváez, Espartero's enemy, and his

army waited just outside the city gates. They had but "one object . . . to get possession of the young Queen." Irving courageously vowed to protect Isabella at all cost. He threw himself into what he imagined to be a life or death situation and dictated a letter to all the foreign diplomats in Madrid, inviting them to join him in an expedition to the palace. It was their plan, upon the arrival of the rebel army, to offer their protection to the Queen and demand that Narváez not touch her. Much to the disappointment of the diplomatic corps, Her Gracious Majesty "respectfully declined" their gallant offer of protection. Narváez was not her enemy, as they had assumed, but a clever strategist who planned the overthrow of Espartero in order to join forces with the Queen. What had promised to be a bloody battle between the troops of Espartero and Narváez deteriorated into a comic-opera scene. Espartero was defeated—politically, not by guns or cannon—and left Spain quietly.

When the United States recognized the Narváez government, Irving had completed his first year of service as Minister to Spain. He had been periodically so ill during his first six months in Madrid that at times he could not dictate his reports to Secretary of State Daniel Webster in Washington. Irving would have resigned his post because of his illness, but he knew a change of ministers at this critical period would have been detrimental to American interests in Spain. Besides, he was too much in need of the large salary attached to the post to give it up.

"The poet, Irving," as he was affectionately known in Madrid, was now the seasoned diplomat. Even Daniel Webster was known to lay aside all other matters to read Irving's finely composed dispatches immediately upon their arrival.

Irving became so completely immersed in the intrigues of international politics that he did not have the time or opportunity to do the writing he had planned. The biography of Washington, and another to be titled *Mahomet and His Successors*, remained untouched until his last year in Spain. With his embassy staff away for the summer and affairs between Spain and America at almost a standstill, he was free to pore over his notes on Washington and Mahomet. His pleasure in literary work was revived, and he wrote a friend:

"In the early part of my literary career I used to think I would take warning by the fate of writers who worked until they 'wrote themselves down,' and that I would retire while still in the freshness of my powers, but you see circumstances have obliged me to change my plan and I am likely to write on until the pen drops from my hand."

Irving resigned as Minister to Spain in April, 1846. His return to the United States was the subject of some note. The poet Longfellow even read with interest the newspaper report of his arrival in Boston on the ship "Cambriar" on September 18, 1846. More important to Irving and his family was the fact that he was back home at Sunnyside. "Never," he rejoiced, "did an old bachelor come to such a loving home." His nieces were there to smother him with affection and care for his every need. No effort was spared to make their uncle happy. His nephew, Pierre Munro Irving, who became his secretary, was also there. Pierre's main duty was to shield Irving from the all-too-curious world beyond the peaceful boundaries of Sunnyside. Pierre also managed his uncle's financial affairs, relieving the still hard-working writer of that responsibility. Because of the heavy financial burdens which Irving had assumed for Ebenezer's daughters, it was necessary for him to continue to write to the very end of his life.

Three biographies remained to be completed: *Oliver Goldsmith* (1846), which Irving had begun in Paris in the 1820's, *Mahomet and His Successors* (1850), and *The Life of George Washington*. The biography of Washington was to be his longest work and the one for which he hoped to be remembered as a writer. Although Irving had decided to write the biography as early as 1825, it was 1855 before the first volume of his five-volume portrait of the first President was published and 1859 when the fifth and final volume appeared. Irving's preparation of the manuscript, which for years after it was published was accepted as the most complete and authoritative biography of Washington, was almost reverent. He worked inexhaustibly to create a living portrait of Washington; he wanted to present Washington the man, not an artificial concept of him. He wrote in simple language which the average citizen would enjoy reading. He felt his goal had been achieved when a friend told him he had read sections of the work to his children, who enjoyed it thoroughly. Irving exclaimed:

"That's it: that is what I write it for. I want it so clear that anybody can understand it. I want the action to shine through the style. No style, indeed; no encumbrance of ornament . . . ."

Washington Irving was the first native American author to have his works characterized as classic literature. His colorful legends of the Hudson River Valley helped awaken Americans to an appreciation of their nation and its native literature. His stories based on the legends of Europe and Spain gave his readers a glimpse of the world beyond their own shores. Irving's popularity as a writer was so widespread in his later years that his influence on the whole of American literature cannot be overestimated.

Longfellow, Emerson, and Hawthorne acknowledged their close study of his work and its influence on their writing. Edgar Allan Poe's admiration of Irving's books, though tinged with envy, was so great that it inspired him to send the mature author the manuscript of his story "The Fall of the House of Usher." Irving, who had on occasion hidden behind the literary aliases of Jonathan Oldstyle, Diedrich Knickerbocker, Geoffrey Crayon, and Fray Antonio Agapida, even enjoyed the ultimate compliment of having it rumored that Sir Walter Scott was the author of *The Sketch-Book*.

Washington Irving died on November 28, 1859, but he left Oldstyle, Knickerbocker, Crayon, and Agapida to live on forever.

Suggested Reading*

IRVING'S TALES AND OTHER PROSE:

Adventures of Captain Bonneville. Illus. Portland, Ore.: Binfords & Mort, 1954.

Astoria. Illus. Portland, Ore.: Binfords & Mort, 1967.

Bracebridge Hall; or, The Humorists. St. Clair Shores, Mich.: Scholarly Press, reprint.†

Chronicle of The Conquest of Granada, A. 2 vols. New York: AMS Press, reprint.†

History of New York . . . by Diedrich Knickerbocker, A. New Haven: College & University Press, 1964.

Life of George Washington. Edited by Jess Stein. New York: Sleepy Hollow Press.†

Mahomet and His Successors. Edited by E. M. Feltskog and H. A. Pochmann. Madison, Wisc.: University of Wisconsin Press, 1970.

Rip Van Winkle and The Legend of Sleepy Hollow. New York: The Macmillan Co., 1963.

Sketch Book of Geoffrey Crayon, Gent., The. New York: E. P. Dutton & Co.†

Tales of the Alhambra. New York: Avon Books, 1970.

Tales of a Traveller. Freeport, N.Y.: Books for Libraries.†

Tour on the Prairies. New York: Pantheon Books, 1967.

BOOKS ABOUT IRVING'S LIFE AND TIMES:

Benet, Laura, *Washington Irving.* New York: Dodd, Mead & Co., 1944.

Bolton, Sarah K., *Famous American Authors.* New York: Thomas Y. Crowell Co., 1954.

Brooks, Van Wyck, *The World of Washington Irving.* New York: E. P. Dutton & Co., 1950.

Seton, Anya, *Washington Irving.* Illustrated by Harve Stein. Boston: Houghton Mifflin Co.†

Wood, James P., *Sunnyside: A Life of Washington Irving.* New York: Pantheon Books, 1967.

* The author has listed popular editions for convenient reference.
† Publication date not listed.

James Fenimore Cooper

James Fenimore Cooper
/ Ardent American

   In 1832, a year before his return from Europe, James Fenimore Cooper received a letter from his nephew, Richard Cooper, a lawyer in Cooperstown, New York. The letter reported that Otsego Hall, the Cooper family home, was still standing but that it was deserted and had fallen into a state of disrepair. The mansion, surrounded by several acres of land, was a third of a century old and had been built by the novelist's father, William Cooper, the founder of Cooperstown. Otsego Hall, as it came to be known while Judge Cooper was alive, was no longer owned by the Cooper family. It had been sold in the 1820's to satisfy debts against the Cooper estate.

   As Cooper read the letter from Richard, his thoughts drifted back to his family home. He lapsed into a reflective mood and considered the possibility of returning to Cooperstown. He would need a permanent place of residence for his family when they returned to America. Why not buy the old mansion and restore it to its original splendor? The further challenge of regaining the respect and authority once commanded by the Cooper name and the fortune amassed by his father held even greater appeal. The fortune had been lost through mismanagement and careless spending, but that, too, could be reestablished.

   Cooper immediately wrote to his nephew and instructed him to investigate the possibility of purchasing the old mansion at a reasonable price. He knew that restoration of the house, which had stood vacant since about 1820, would require a large amount of money. Negotiations for purchase were not completed until

1834, at which time Cooper launched an extensive remodeling based on plans drawn by his close friend, Samuel Morse, the inventor of the telegraph.

The letter to Richard turned Cooper's memories back to his childhood, when Cooperstown had recently been carved out of the wilderness by his father. The small settlement was nestled on the shores of Lake Otsego, located in upstate New York, then the western frontier of civilization in the northern part of the United States. William Cooper, in his book *The Guide in the Wilderness*, made the observation that this frontier was settled by many New England people who were well educated and willing workers in their newfound home.

William Cooper had come from Burlington, New Jersey, in 1786. He purchased forty thousand acres on the shores of Lake Otsego with the intent of pioneering this northern part of New York State. This was three years before the birth of his eleventh child, James, on September 15, 1789. Fenimore was not added to Cooper's name until he was thirty-seven years old. This change was made when he petitioned the state legislature for permission to legally change his name to James Fenimore in order to become a direct male heir to his mother's estate. There were no male heirs left to carry on the name Fenimore, and since his mother owned property in her own right it was her wish that one of her sons take the name for this purpose. The legislature turned down his petition to become James Fenimore, but on April 13, 1826, granted him permission to legally change his name to James Fenimore Cooper.

In November, 1790, when the infant James was thirteen months old, his father moved the family from Burlington to the new and sparsely populated settlement of Cooperstown. Mrs. Cooper was extremely unhappy over this move to the isolated wilderness, but her husband had been dividing his time between Burlington and Cooperstown since 1786 and felt it was necessary to settle permanently in his newly established village.

The growth of Cooperstown out of the wilderness was rapid. From the sound of the first axe felling trees for temporary shelter the venture was successful. William Cooper was clever and resourceful in attracting settlers to the remote frontier. He made the terms offered to new settlers extremely attractive. He sold land to them at reasonable prices with low interest rates on their mortgages.

To further spur productive efforts among the settlers William Cooper set up a simple economic system. He established a community store, from which the settlers could buy their supplies on credit. He also built a warehouse and shipped in grain, sugar, potash kettles, and farming equipment. When the farms carved from the wilderness around the village began to be productive, he bought the maple sugar, potash, and other products from the farmers. Much of this primitive farming depended upon the natural resources found there, such as the sap from maple trees, which was made into sugar.

William Cooper's private fortune grew as rapidly as the town he founded. As was the custom in new settlements, he was soon elected, unofficially, to fill the highest judicial office in Cooperstown and was forever thereafter known by the honorary title of "Judge." The hastily constructed log cabin he built for his family just before their arrival in the village was soon replaced by a comfortable manor house. In 1799, just thirteen years after Cooper had begun his frontier venture, he moved his family into a fine mansion constructed from handmade brick. The house, Otsego Hall, occupied a prominent parcel of ground on the lake and dominated the town.

Judge Cooper continued to expand his property holdings. He became one of the wealthiest and most influential men in the state. His children enjoyed the best of everything, even though their home was situated in a small village in the midst of the frontier wilderness. Their father's skill as a developer and manager eliminated many of the discomforts usually experienced by a pioneer family in remote territory.

Young James was a gray-eyed, light-haired boy, whose ruddy complexion reflected the outdoor life he loved. He possessed an instinctive understanding of the wilderness and fitted easily into frontier life. As next to the youngest of the Cooper children (a twelfth child was born after the move to Cooperstown), he actually enjoyed more of the advantages of his father's position than his older brothers, who had been required to assume responsibilities immediately upon their arrival in the new settlement.

James's first teacher was his older sister Hannah, who had reached young womanhood while he was still a little boy. Hannah taught him the alphabet and simple arithmetic. Later he was enrolled in a one-room school that was established in the village's only public building. The same building also served as town hall, courthouse, ballroom on Saturday night, and church on Sunday morning.

James showed no signs of exceptional intelligence or creative ability. He was an average boy and enjoyed the rugged outdoor life of a pioneer. His friends included trappers, hunters, and trail blazers. Thus James was not unlike the character who would appear and reappear in the pages of his Leatherstocking books under the names of Natty Bumppo, Leatherstocking, Hawkeye, Pathfinder, Deerslayer, and the trapper.

James very much preferred the outdoor life to books. He had even appeared slow in comprehending the little he was taught at home and at the Cooperstown school. His parents began to doubt seriously whether he would ever develop an ability to learn in depth any one subject or skill. But since he was the son of a wealthy man, all the proper steps were taken to develop any ability he might possess.

When James was ten years old, Judge Cooper sent him to Albany, New York. Here he was prepared for entrance into college. He studied under the rector of St. Peter's Episcopal Church. At this time James Cooper showed no promise for a literary career. It was even painful to watch him in the act of writing: he held his pen awkwardly and begrudged every moment he spent in the exercise of penmanship. He read just enough to pass his examinations.

Yet James possessed one desire totally out of keeping with what then appeared to be his nature: he said he wanted to write a story someday. This was no doubt boyish chatter, although it is tempting to read into it an unconscious awareness of his potential creative ability.

Despite his slowness, James was ready to enter Yale University by the time he was thirteen years old, not an early age to begin college at that time. In America at the turn of the nineteenth century, a college course did not include much more than what is now offered by a good preparatory school.

James was expelled from Yale at the end of his sophomore year. Though the cause remains a mystery, several stories have been told concerning his dismissal. One is about an unpopular professor who, upon entering his classroom one morning, found that he had been "replaced" by a donkey tied into the chair behind his desk. Another tells of a feud that James had been carrying on with a classmate. An explosion took place late one night in the room of this boy, and James was said to be the prime suspect, if not the guilty party. But whatever the reason for his expulsion from Yale, Cooper bore no ill will against the school, though he had little to say in its favor.

James was not yet sixteen when he was dismissed from Yale. His father decided that for the time being the best place for him was at home, where he remained for two years. As far as James was concerned, he was finished with books; he wanted nothing further to do with them, either for study or for entertainment. The next step was to find an occupation that would have as little to do with books as possible.

Since his family was wealthy, there was no demand on James to enter a trade. He had no need to create an income. His life would eventually be taken up in the management of his share of his father's estate. But he needed an occupation until he reached maturity. The United States Navy offered the best prospect to a relatively well-educated young man. The Academy at Annapolis had not yet been founded. The only way James could prepare to become a naval officer was to serve aboard a merchant vessel for a year or two. He signed on the "Sterling," a freight vessel which sailed in the fall of 1806 from Wiscasset, Maine, carrying a cargo of flour bound for England. James sailed before the mast as an able-bodied seaman. One day he would write in the preface of his novel, *Ned Myers; or, A Life Before the Mast*:

In the year 1806, the editor, then a lad, fresh from Yale, and destined for the navy, made his first voyage in a merchantman, with a view to get some practical knowledge of his profession. This was the fashion of the day, though its utility, on the whole, may very well be questioned. The voyage was a long one . . . extending to near the close of the year 1807.

Upon Cooper's return to the United States he received his commission in the Navy. It was during his naval service that Cooper developed the resentment toward the English that was to remain with him all his life. The cause of his resentment was "crimping," or forcing men to serve in the Navy against their will. The British Navy practiced crimping against American sailors.

Cooper related two such incidents in *Ned Myers*. He told of two sailors with whom he served who were taken against their will. One of these men was taken from the ship as it lay at anchor off Cowes, England. The Captain and most of the crew had gone ashore, leaving a few men on board to maintain the vessel, when a British cutter came alongside. An officer from the cutter came aboard and forced one of the Americans to leave the ship with him. The officer also attempted to force another sailor to leave with him, but this man had a certificate which stated that he had been discharged from the British Navy after a long term of service. This certificate was his legal protection. A few days later he applied at Somerset House, British Naval Headquarters in London, for some money owed him. The clerk requested that he leave his certificate so that his record could be searched out. The sailor was followed after he left the office and taken by the British authorities. He no longer had his certificate in hand to prove his immunity. Neither of these American sailors was ever seen or heard from again.

In 1808 Cooper was one of a small group of men under the command of a Lieutenant Woolsey, who was sent to develop a squadron of ships to patrol the Great Lakes. "Lieutenant . . . Woolsey . . . ," Cooper was to write in his naval history, "was empowered to make contracts for the construction of three vessels, one . . . to be built on Lake Ontario . . . the other two on Lake Champlain."

The expansion of the United States as an international power and her increasing disagreements with England made it necessary to deploy warships on these inland waters. England had already placed warships on Lake Ontario and Lake Erie. Cooper later described the activities of this small group of American officers in his book *The History of the Navy of the United States of America*, published in 1839.

After a long winter in this remote outpost, the officers were more than ready for a change of pace, if not a change of scene. The first vessel was near completion and was to be launched within a short time. The officers decided to celebrate the occasion with a ball. But there was one obstacle. To have a ball there must be ladies present, and there were no ladies available. Everything else was readily obtainable: the refreshments, the music (one of the officers played the fiddle), and even a makeshift ballroom. This would be arranged by converting the mess hall and general dayroom into a ballroom. But finding the ladies was a more difficult problem.

After a campaign carried out with the intensity of a military maneuver and a strategy no less exacting, a number of ladies were located and brought together for the ball. But another problem arose. Since the ladies' dress would by necessity be much less formal than at a military ball in a more populated community, several matters of etiquette remained to be resolved.

Susan Cooper, James's daughter, later recalled her father's story of how Lieutenant Woolsey solved this unusual problem. After a discussion of the situation with his fellow officers, Lieutenant Woolsey evolved a plan of action. Several of the ladies would be wearing shoes and stockings; they were to be led to the head of the Virginia Reel. There were others who would be wearing shoes but no stockings; they were to be placed elsewhere in the dance formation. A third group of ladies would not be wearing shoes or stockings; they were to be led to the foot of the Virgina Reel. A difficult question of northwoods etiquette was thereby resolved, and everyone enjoyed a rare evening of entertainment.

Shortly after the death of his father in 1809, James wrote his brother Richard, now the head of the family, a very intimate letter. James was now a wealthy young man. His career as a naval officer was beginning to place too many restrictions on him. It had been undertaken only as a temporary occupation until his personal business affairs would require his full attention. That time had arrived. More important, he was in love. Susan DeLancey, the object of his affection, demanded a more constant and sustained courtship than the brief furloughs from his remote station on the Great Lakes allowed. He wrote Richard:

Like all the rest of the sons of Adam, I have bowed to the influence of the charms of a fair damsel . . . . I loved her like a man and told her of it like a sailor. . . . As you are coolly to decide, I will as coolly give you the qualities of my mistress; Susan De Lancey is the daughter of a man of very respectable connections and a handsome fortune

—amiable, sweet tempered and happy in her disposition. She has been educated in the country, occasionally trying the temperature of the City to rub off the rust—but hold a moment; it is enough she pleases *me* in the qualities of her *person* and *mind*.

On January 1, 1811, just three years after he had been appointed to the Navy, Cooper married Susan at her home in Westchester County, New York. He resigned from the Navy in May of the same year, at the end of a year-long furlough taken for the purpose of courting Susan. After several years of moving between Cooperstown and Westchester, the couple settled at Angevine Farm in Westchester. This property belonged to Susan, and on it Cooper built a house. But there was a constant pull between Westchester and Cooperstown. James's share in his father's estate demanded his presence in Cooperstown, while Susan's love for her family drew her back to Westchester.

Angevine Farm was near the town of Scarsdale in Westchester County, not far from the DeLancey home. The Coopers lived there from 1818 until 1822. Although living in Scarsdale made it difficult for Cooper to care for his portion of his father's estate, he was faithful in his management of his affairs. His mother had died in 1817, eight years after the death of his father. Two years later, his last surviving older brother, William, died, leaving Cooper to manage the family's financial affairs. His brothers had been poor managers. The larger part of the estate to which they were heirs fell into disrepair because they had not understood the necessity of maintaining property and keeping it free of debt. Cooper could not be blamed for their mismanagement.

It became his responsibility to manage what was left of the ruined estate. As administrator he had to produce the money required to pay off the many claims accumulated against the estate since his father's death. He was also burdened with the responsibility of supporting his brothers' widows and minor children and paying his brothers' personal debts. These finan-

cial demands, added to Cooper's own generous habits of spending, would keep him on the brink of bankruptcy for most of his
life, in spite of his large income.

Cooper needed money and embraced every opportunity to
increase his income. He had turned a substantial profit when he
introduced Merino sheep into the United States. His potato
crops and a cotton brokerage venture had also paid well. These
investments left him with a large sum of cash which he wanted
to reinvest instead of spending immediately. The whaling industry offered an opportunity to do so.

Cooper purchased a three-quarter interest in a whaling ship,
the "Union," an old but seaworthy craft. She made three voyages within one year, the time most whalers took to make one
voyage. Cooper occasionally gave himself the pleasure of sailing
with the "Union" from New York City to Rhode Island, where
she launched forth into the Atlantic in search of whales.

Like his father, Cooper was stimulated by having multiple
business interests. Unlike his father, he did not economize. Yet
with all his financial problems Cooper always found time for a
few hours of relaxation after the evening meal. He enjoyed reading aloud to Susan after the children were tucked into bed. His
attitude toward books had changed with the years. He now
found much pleasure in reading history books and biographies
of famous people. Shakespeare and the poets also took their place
among the selections he read aloud.

One evening Cooper read to Susan from a new romance just
arrived from England. After several chapters, he threw the book
aside, declaring that he could probably write a more interesting
book himself. Susan found the idea amusing, so to prove his
point Cooper sat down at the desk and began a novel.

Cooper became so engrossed in the project that it forced everything else from his mind. He first outlined a tentative plot. Then
he conferred with his wife on the details of each character and
phase of the story. It was his intention to imitate the style, con-

tent, and characters of an English romance. Therefore he laid the scene in England. The fact that Cooper had spent very little time there and was totally unfamiliar with English life made no difference to him. The entire project was, at this juncture, nothing more than a stunt, even though he was momentarily pouring all his energy into it.

Discouragement soon set in. The idea of writing any kind of book, let alone a novel, became ridiculous to him. But Susan, who had at first been amused by the entire project, was not to be put off. She had begun to perceive the possibilities in the part of the work he had completed. She insisted that he finish and then publish it. Cooper couldn't take seriously the idea of seeing his novel in print, but he was willing to do anything to please his beloved wife.

It was not surprising that he was pleased by his wife's enthusiasm. He was thirty years old and had never felt at home with a pen in his hand. The only spark of creativity he had ever expressed was in verse. To satisfy the request of a wandering ballad singer many years before he had written a ballad, "Burnt Buffalo." From time to time throughout his youth and young manhood he had contributed bits of verse to the Cooperstown newspaper, but he had long since abandoned verse writing.

Before Cooper took the manuscript to the printer, he read a portion of it to a small group of friends. They were not told who had written it. Much to Cooper's delight, one woman insisted that she had heard the manuscript read before, but not by Cooper, and that it had been written by a woman. Nothing could have been more encouraging to Cooper. His entire effort had been to imitate the popular sentimentality of the Romantic period, when many novels were written by women. This listener's reaction proved the success of his efforts.

Precaution was published anonymously in 1820. No one suspected that it had been written by a man, least of all by Squire James Fenimore Cooper of Angevine Farm. Cooper was surprised to find that his novel was not only well received in America but also printed in a pirated edition in England and given some critical comment.

Little can be said for *Precaution* except that it served to goad Cooper on to more substantial literary effort. The novel actually became an embarrassment to him because of its sentimental tone. He therefore settled down to more serious writing and produced *The Spy* (1821). In the Introduction to this second novel he expressed the hope that it would be "more worthy of the favor" of the public than his first novel.

The Spy, like all Cooper's novels, was published anonymously. The title page stated only that it had been written by a gentleman of New York. At that time it was considered crude and ungentlemanly to write for money, whether the work was a book or a newspaper article. It was for this reason that Sir Walter Scott remained anonymous and Washington Irving chose to masquerade as Oldstyle, Knickerbocker, Geoffrey Crayon, or Agapida.

At the time Cooper began writing there was no international copyright law to protect authors from pirated editions in other countries. The only way an American or English author could protect his work from being pirated, and this only temporarily, was to have it published simultaneously in England and America. In this way the author received a large share of the profits before a pirated edition could appear. A pirated edition usually sold for a much lower price than the authorized edition.

In an effort to avoid having other works pirated as *Precaution* had been, Cooper enlisted the services of Washington Irving. Irving was then living in England. Through Irving's efforts, *The Spy* was published in an authorized London edition, which meant that the words "Author's Edition" were printed on the title page. This informed the purchaser that the author was receiving the royalties. Even so, *The Spy* was pirated many times over.

Cooper was well into the writing of his third novel when he decided to change the family residence from Angevine Farm to New York City. In the city, the Coopers settled in a commodious house owned by Mrs. Cooper's father. There were two reasons for their move. The educational needs of their son and four daughters demanded more suitable facilities than were available in Scarsdale, and Cooper wanted to be close to the center of the publishing industry.

Cooper's career as a writer was now moving forward at full tilt. Authorship proved so lucrative that he gave up all his other business activities except his farms and real estate holdings. He now devoted all his time to writing. Since he published his own books, he had to live as close to the printing office as possible. He sold his books directly to the bookshops. Even in later years, when he lived in Europe, he published his books himself. He printed editions of individual works in England, France, and Germany.

Cooper's romance, *The Pioneers*, was published in 1823. A year later, in 1824, he published *The Pilot*, the first sea story to be written by an American author.

Cooper's early work as a writer was carried out during the late Romantic Movement in English and European literature. Among the main elements of the Romantic Movement in English literature were simplicity of expression, a love of untouched nature, an increased awareness of the past, and a rejection of materialistic values. The Romanticist displayed a renewed appreciation of the common or natural man.

Cooper's Leatherstocking novels are a perfect example of Romantic literature in America. These five novels, *The Pioneers* (1823), *The Last of the Mohicans* (1826), and *The Prairie* (1827), written during this period, and *The Pathfinder* (1840) and *The Deerslayer* (1841), written after his return from Europe, contain many of the elements of the Romantic Movement outlined above. The English and European writers of the Romantic Period consciously put these elements into their works. The Romanticism of Cooper's novels was the natural outgrowth of his pioneer background, of his love for and familiarity with the unspoiled wilderness of the American frontier and the men who pioneered it. His character Hawkeye in *The Last of the Mohicans* was a perfect example of the western man who had broken away from the artificiality of civilization. He was the common man represented by the Romantic Movement; the man who expressed the kindliness, wisdom, bravery, and rustic chivalry idealized by the writers of this period. Chingachgook, Hawkeye's Indian companion, was Cooper's conception of the natural man, or noble savage, idealized by the Romantic writers. Chingachgook reflected the native intelligence, loyalty, and fraternal love known only to those unspoiled by civilization.

After the publication in 1826 of *The Last of the Mohicans*, his most popular book, Cooper took his family to Europe. This was an unusual thing for a husband and father of this period to do. Most American men preferred to make their visits to Europe without their families. But Cooper was too involved in the joys of family life to leave his wife and children at home. Not only did his party include Mrs. Cooper, their son James Fenimore, and four daughters, but also his nephew William, whom he had adopted, and several servants.

The Coopers sailed for Europe in June, 1826. Cooper took with him the unfinished manuscript of *The Prairie*. This was the third of the Leatherstocking series. He finished writing it in Europe, and it was published in Paris in 1827. *The Red Rover*, his second sea story, was also published in 1827.

The five years Cooper had planned to live in Europe stretched into seven. At the end of these seven years he was at odds with the governments of France, England, and America. The basis for his disputes was his ardent Americanism in the face of European complacency and ignorance of the New World. Unlike other American writers who traveled in Europe, Cooper was very outspoken about his discontent with things European. Irving, Bryant, Longfellow, and Holmes had all been complimentary in their written and spoken opinions of what they observed during their visits abroad.

Cooper particularly disliked the English. He made clear his disapproval of the American idolization of all that was English. He went to great lengths to magnify the unattractive features of England as a nation and of the English people. He never missed an opportunity to point out the conditions that brought on the American Revolution. His book *Notions of the Americans; Picked Up by a Traveling Bachelor*, published in London and Philadelphia in 1828, offended the English because of its uncomplimentary portrayal of them.

Cooper's hostility toward everything that suggested monarchical government distressed those in high places in America as well as abroad. Many Americans of the nineteenth century still cherished an affection for the idea of monarchy. They resented Cooper's open praise of his country's republican form of government and especially his claim that America was not only the equal of all great nations but superior to England, her mother country.

While Cooper was living in France he unintentionally became embroiled in French politics. General Lafayette, leader of the French liberal party, suggested that certain changes be made in the French economic system. Louis Phillippe, the Citizen King, saw in this situation the opportunity he had been waiting for to force Lafayette out of public life. He turned the affair into a public test of popularity. Louis used every means within his power to undermine the General's influence over the French people. It was his plan to discredit Lafayette's premise that the economy of the United States was a more practical and substantial system than that of France.

Cooper and Lafayette had been friends for many years. In this crisis Lafayette turned to Cooper for confirmation of his concept of the United States' financial system. Cooper did not want to become involved in what he realized was a French domestic affair, over which even the French press was divided. But Lafayette was anxious to defend his point, and finally prevailed upon Cooper to write a pamphlet which would clarify the economic system of the United States. It did not appear to Cooper that this would be taking sides in the affair.

When the pamphlet appeared, the French newspapers and all others concerned accepted Cooper's explanation of the American economy. Lafayette's position was then understood and public controversy over the matter subsided. Cooper later wrote a series of articles for a French newspaper, further explaining points in the United States' economy.

No actual changes in the French economy resulted from this controversy. The matter probably would have been forgotten had not another American also felt it necessary to write a pamphlet on the American economy. The author of this pamphlet was Leavitt Harris, one-time Secretary to the American Legation in St. Petersburg, Russia, now attached to the American Ministry in Paris. In his pamphlet he disputed Cooper's facts and figures. He also declared himself a monarchist.

Cooper responded in a short, mild letter which was published in a Paris newspaper. He considered the matter closed. But not long afterwards, President Andrew Jackson appointed Harris Chargé d'Affaires of the American Ministry in Paris. At about the same time, the United States Department of State published an account of government expenses based on state figures rather than federal figures. This report gave ammunition to critics who had said that Cooper's figures were inaccurate, even though his statement had been based, correctly, on federal figures.

This series of events was not a deliberate attempt by the Jackson Administration to discredit Cooper, but rather the poorly timed actions and blunders of the American bureaucratic government. But the American press seized upon this unfortunate series of events to make Cooper appear guilty of interfering in French affairs and of making a vulgar show of his patriotism.

In self-defense, Cooper wrote a letter to the American people, which was published in a Philadelphia newspaper. In this letter he explained his original reason for having written the pamphlet published in France. Much to his amazement, he was condemned further by the American press. This attack set the tone for his future relationship with the American press, which even at this period in American history was a formidable adversary. But Cooper would use this turmoil to his best advantage, in spite of the havoc it brought to his own life. He was not one to back away from a fight, however great the odds against him.

Not all newspapermen were against Cooper. A few, including Samuel Morse and his brother, who together owned and operated the *New York Observer*, took Cooper's side. In 1833, Samuel Morse wrote his brother from Paris that Cooper was extremely popular in Europe:

I have visited, in Europe, many countries, and what I have asserted of the fame of Mr. Cooper I assert from personal knowledge. In every city of Europe that I visited the works of Cooper were conspicuously placed in the windows of every bookshop. They are published, as soon as he produces them, in thirty-four different places in Europe.

Cooper's main objective in going abroad had been to write. But his outspoken convictions, reflected in his conversation as well as his books, cost him much in money and popularity. This is not to say that he was unpopular with the people of Europe as a whole. His books were published and sold in more than thirty European cities. They were also translated into thirty different languages, including Turkish. But the constant criticism, both of his books and of his patriotic activities, placed him on the defensive at home and abroad. His sentiments took on Hawkeye's tone in *The Last of the Mohicans*:

I am not a prejudiced man, nor one who vaunts himself on his natural privileges . . . and I am willing to own that my people have many ways, of which, as an honest man, I can't approve. It is one of their customs to write in books what they have done and seen, instead of telling them in their villages, where the lie can be given to the face of a cowardly boaster, and the brave soldier can call on his comrades to witness for the truth of his words. . . . But every story has its two sides . . . .

These words of Hawkeye to Chingachgook were prophetic of Cooper's personal life, which was to have "two sides." There was the image created by the American press to sell newspapers and entertain readers with colorful reports on Cooper's so-called eccentric activities in Europe. The other side of Cooper's life revealed a man so patriotic that he was willing to sacrifice his career as a writer rather than abandon his principles as a United States citizen.

The Cooper family returned to America on November 5, 1833. Cooper was a much more serious man than he had been when he left for Europe seven years earlier. He was not in the mood for a ceremonious welcome home like that which had been given to Irving a short time before. A parade and a number of speeches, banquets, and receptions had been planned in his honor, and he did not realize that they were sincere symbols of welcome from his fellow countrymen. The memory of the vicious attacks from the American press over his involvement in the French financial controversy still lingered in his mind. He had incorrectly assumed that the attacks by the press represented the feelings of the American people as a whole. Actually, these attacks by the press reflected the thinking of only a small segment of the people. But Cooper had become so biased in his thinking about the situation that he stubbornly refused to accept the gestures of welcome offered him. Among those who were to lead these ceremonies were many old friends such as William Cullen Bryant, Peter Jay, Dr. John W. Francis, Jeremiah Van Rensselaer, and others, all respected citizens of the city. Cooper mistakenly thought that these people had imagined themselves victims of two of his recent books, *The Bravo*, published in 1831, and *The Headsman*, 1833, and were being hypocritical by taking part in the official welcome home ceremonies.

In the spring of 1834, Cooper published what purported to be his farewell to the public as a writer: *A Letter to His Countrymen*. Strangely enough, this slim volume was the first of his books ever to carry his name on the title page. Its message was aimed at the American press, and he remarked in closing:

The American who wishes to illustrate and enforce the peculiar principles of his own country, by the agency of polite literature, will, for a long time to come, I fear, find that *his* constituency . . . is still too much under the influence of foreign theories, to receive him with favor. It is under this conviction that I lay aside the pen.

In spite of his dramatic farewell in *A Letter to His Countrymen*, neither Cooper nor his pen stayed in retirement for long. Cooper was too much the literary lion to retire so easily and so early in life. He was forty-five when he wrote and published *A Letter to His Countrymen*. Considering his normally aggressive nature, this book was somewhat out of character for him. But he was feeling sorry for himself at the time because of the unfair treatment he had received from the American press. As it turned out, *A Letter to His Countrymen* was nothing more than a formal conclusion to the first phase of his literary career. His most sophisticated work was still to follow.

In July, 1835, *The Monikins*, a satire, was published. During the two years that followed, Cooper published five volumes on his travels in Europe.

After spending several winters in New York City, the Coopers settled permanently in Cooperstown in 1836. They had spent the summers there since their return from Europe. Cooper had accumulated a small but adequate amount of money on which he and his family could live comfortably, and the prospect of once again becoming a country squire was appealing.

But Cooper's return to Cooperstown was not the happy occasion he might have expected it to be. The town had not expanded in size, but most of the people he had known there were gone. In their place he found strangers. Few smiles greeted him and his family as they moved through the streets to Otsego Hall. Even more disappointing was the fact that his father, William Cooper, founder and chief benefactor of the town, appeared to have been forgotten. His memory and the traditions for which he stood were buried with the past.

Although Cooper was disappointed to find his family name almost forgotten in Cooperstown, he and his family settled into Otsego Hall and were comfortable in the knowledge that they were really home at last.

Cooper published two books, *The American Democrat* and *The Chronicles of Cooperstown* in 1838, both written after his return to Cooperstown.

Then began an unfortunate series of events. Cooper's nephew Richard, with whom he had communicated in 1832 about the restoration of Otsego Hall, had begun work according to his uncle's directions. But the grounds were in a deplorable condition when Cooper returned. They had been used as a playground, picnic ground, and general thoroughfare by the people of Cooperstown. As soon as Cooper began the work of restoring the grounds around the mansion, he closed them to the public. This brought about much resentment from the townspeople. He was accused of undemocratic action toward his neighbors and fellow citizens.

Three Mile Point, or Myrtle Grove, as it was also called, belonged to the parcel of land on which Otsego Hall was built. Unlike Otsego Hall, Three Mile Point had never passed out of the Cooper family's ownership. But after Otsego Hall had passed into other hands and then become vacant, Three Mile Point had fallen into public use. It was no longer considered private property by the people of Cooperstown. Although William Cooper had allowed the townspeople limited use of the Point, he had never considered relinquishing ownership of the land.

When informed of the claim made by the public to Three Mile
Point, Cooper published a statement in the local newspaper as-
serting his ownership of the land. He based his claim on a clause
in his father's will. He then dismissed the subject from his mind.
But the citizens of Cooperstown were unwilling to let the matter
rest. They were determined to win their objective. They held a
town meeting and voted to ignore Cooper's published statement
of ownership. A set of resolutions was drawn up against Cooper.
One of them recommended that the trustees of the Cooperstown
library remove all his books from its shelves.

It was at this time that Cooper put his view of the Three Mile
Point controversy and the events leading up to it into his two
novels, *Homeward Bound* and *Home as Found*, both published
in 1838. He felt that his point in the dispute had been won by the
fact that he did own the land in question. If he had not been a
successful author, a democrat in a hotbed of Whigs, and out of
favor with the press, the dispute would more than likely have
faded into oblivion. But the two Cooperstown newspapers could
not resist mentioning the Three Mile Point affair, and the national Whig press snapped it up.

Cooper was accused of persecuting the people of his village
because he would not allow them free use of Three Mile Point.
Once again the press conspired to disparage him. This time they
had mistaken their man. Cooper initiated legal action against
several editors who had published abusive articles. He asked
these editors to publish corrections of their misstatements. They
refused. He sued them for libel and won.

There followed six years of successive libel suits which Cooper
brought against various newspaper editors. One of the reasons
the newspapers were so quick to pounce on him over the Three
Mile Point dispute stemmed from a remark made in the Introduction to his novel *The Heidenmauer*, which had been published in 1832. He described a journey which he took through a
section of Belgium where a battle had been fought only a week
earlier. According to newspaper reports, the Dutch troops, who

were the aggressors, had committed unwarranted acts of war in the area, leaving it in ruins. When Cooper arrived there he said that he could find no evidence of conditions as reported by the newspapers. Disgusted with such irresponsible reporting, he clearly indicated his feelings, stirring the ire of the European and American press. "Each hour, as life advances," he commented, "am I made to see how capricious and vulgar is the immortality conferred by a newspaper!"

The press thereafter never missed an opportunity to discredit Cooper. The Three Mile Point dispute was nothing more than a local affair. It probably would have remained just that had not the press chosen to use it as a vehicle for misinformation. Distinguished citizens throughout the United States were shocked by the vicious attacks on Cooper. But no one defended him publicly, although many encouraged him from a safe distance and congratulated him on his victories.

Editor Horace Greeley attempted to persuade Cooper to drop his legal action against the newspapers. He wanted Cooper to confine his battle to the columns of the *New York Tribune*, which he offered for the purpose. Greeley was always anxious to keep his readers panting after the *Tribune*'s next edition. He saw in the Three Mile Point dispute an unparalleled opportunity for a long series of front-page news features calculated to keep newspaper sales at fever pitch. But Cooper had decided on his own plan of action and the *Tribune* did not fit into it.

Cooper began an intensive study of New York State law, specifically libel laws. He became so well informed that he was later considered the first authority in this branch of state law. After he absorbed all he could, Cooper enlisted the services of his nephew, Richard Cooper, a lawyer. Together they entered the courts, Cooper leading the arguments against the defendants. Richard acted more as an adviser and aide than as a lawyer to his uncle, who conducted several of these cases alone. Cooper possessed an unusual talent for legal argument. In a case which pertained to his *Naval History*, he spoke unceasingly for six hours. His argument was so interestingly presented that not one person left the courtroom during the entire discourse.

Cooper won most of his cases, although the press ignored his victories. But the very fact that he had won was inspiration enough to renew his creative energies. He wrote a novel, *Mercedes of Castile*, in 1840, before his legal battles had reached their fever pitch. In the midst of his most violent battles with the press, the genius which Cooper thought had forsaken him again came to life. In rapid succession he wrote six new novels: *The Pathfinder* (1840), *The Deerslayer* (1841), *The Two Admirals* (1842), *Wing-and-Wing* (1842), *Wyandotté* (1843), and *Afloat and Ashore* (1844).

The Pathfinder and *The Deerslayer* completed Cooper's series of Leatherstocking novels which he had begun eighteen years before with *The Pioneers*. *The Last of the Mohicans* and *The Prairie* were the second and third novels in this series.

During this period of courtroom action, Cooper wrote five other novels. They were *Miles Wallingford* (1844), *Satanstoe* (1845), *The Chainbearer* (1845), *The Redskins* (1846), and *The Crater* (1847).

Satanstoe was the first in a series known as the Littlepage novels, which included also *The Chainbearer* and *The Redskins*. In these three novels Cooper traced the deterioration of the principle of private land ownership in the United States.

Even though the critical comment on the books Cooper wrote during this difficult period was, for the most part, unfavorable, they sold very well. The public loved his books in spite of the efforts of newspaper writers to downgrade them by uncomplimentary reviews.

Lives of Distinguished American Naval Officers, a historical work, was written in 1846, near the close of his court battles.

By 1847 the years of legal conflict in Cooper's life had dropped into the past. His battles with the newspapers had been won, though the victory proved to be a hollow one. He lost more financially in his legal expenses than he gained in principle. Yet Cooper was now at peace. He seemed unconcerned that most of his fortune from his books had been spent during the years of legal conflict.

Cooper settled down contentedly at Cooperstown to live quietly among his neighbors. Cordial relations now reigned between him and his fellow townspeople, though the press at home and abroad still enjoyed taking occasional potshots at him. They published articles from time to time which made it appear that his feud with them and the Three Mile Point dispute were still alive.

In spite of these attacks, Cooper's life now flowed on quietly. His writing became less concerned with material matters and took on a spiritual tone. Cooper, in his late years, drew closer to the Episcopal Church in which he had been reared. Christian allegory became the theme for several of his later novels. This was illustrated in his concern with a Utopian society in *The Crater* (1847) and man's lack of desire for an improved spiritual state in *The Oak Openings* (1848). He pursued this symbolism even further in *The Sea Lions* (1849), in which he used the story to convey his concept of the Christian Trinity.

Cooper had become so engrossed in his current work that he virtually ignored the feelings of ill-will which the newspapers sought to revive. His daughter Susan said that he was content in the joys of his home life. Even while working on a manuscript in his library he insisted that the door be left open that he might hear the comforting sounds of his family going about their daily affairs. He liked to hear the murmured tones of his wife and daughters from different parts of the house. Often he left his desk for a game of backgammon with his wife, or just to talk with the family.

During these quiet years Cooper enjoyed walks around his estate and the village, carriage rides through the country, and boating on Lake Otsego. Although other members of the family and close friends were sometimes invited to join him, he always wanted his wife Susan at his side on these occasions. When she was not along, walks, drives, and lazy boat rides were always cut short by his impatience to get home to Susan.

The last book he published was *The Ways of the Hour* in 1850.

During his life he wrote and published over fifty books and pamphlets.

Although Cooper was an extremely prolific writer, he wrote only one piece of work for the stage, and it was a failure. The play was titled *Upside Down; or, Philosophy in Petticoats.* It was supposed to be a comedy, but Cooper was not a humorist. The play had only three performances in New York City in June, 1850, and then was quietly closed. It was never again staged and never published.

Cooper died September 14, 1851, in Cooperstown. He was writing a book to have been titled *The Towns of Manhattan.* The major portion of this manuscript was complete and probably would have been published after his death, but a few months after Cooper died, the manuscript was almost totally destroyed in a fire. Only a fragment remains.

In a Preface to a late edition of his collected works, Cooper wrote: "If anything from the pen of the writer . . . is . . . to outlive himself, it is, unquestionably, the . . . *Leather-stocking Tales.*" He considered *The Deerslayer* and *The Pathfinder* the best of this series. As if to confirm the author's faith in his work, Balzac, the French writer, called *The Pathfinder* "beautiful—grand, tremendous!" Irving said: "The man who wrote this book is not only a great man, but a good man."

Suggested Reading*

AMONG COOPER'S NOVELS:

Bravo. Edited by Donald Ringe. Masterworks of Literature Series. New Haven, Conn.: College and University Press, 1963.

Chainbearer; or, The Littlepage Manuscripts, The. 2 vols. St. Clair Shores, Mich.: Scholarly Press, reprint, 1969.

Crater; or, Vulcan's Peak, The. Edited by Thomas Philbrick. John Harvard Series. Cambridge, Mass.: Harvard Univ. Press.†

Deerslayer; or, The First War-Path, The. New York: Dodd, Mead & Co., 1952.

Last of the Mohicans; A Narrative of 1757, The. Illus. by N. C. Wyeth. New York: Charles Scribner's Sons, 1952.

Pathfinder; or, The Inland Sea, The. New York: Dodd, Mead & Co., 1953.

Pilot; A Tale of the Sea, The. New York: Dodd, Mead & Co., 1947.

Pioneers; or, The Sources of the Susquehanna: A Descriptive Tale, The. New York: Dodd, Mead & Co., 1958.

Prairie; A Tale, The. New York: Dodd, Mead & Co., 1954.

Precaution; A Novel. St. Clair Shores, Mich.: Scholarly Press, reprint, 1969.

Red Rover, The. Magnolia, Mass.: Peter Smith.†

Satanstoe. Magnolia, Mass.: Peter Smith.†

Sea Lions, The. Edited by Warren S. Walker. Illus. Lincoln, Nebr.: University of Nebraska Press, 1965.

Spy, The. Illus. by Curtis Dahl. New York: Dodd, Mead & Co., 1949.

Water-Witch, The. Illus. New York: AMS Press, 1970.

Wept of Wish-Ton-Wish, The. New York: AMS Press.†

BOOKS ABOUT COOPER:

Boynton, Henry W., *James Fenimore Cooper.* Havertown, Pa.: Richard West, reprint, 1973.

Cantwell, Robert, *Famous Men of Letters.* New York: Dodd, Mead & Co., 1959.

Lounsbury, Thomas R., *James Fenimore Cooper.* Havertown, Pa.: Richard West, reprint, 1973.

* The author has listed popular editions for convenient reference.
† Publication date not listed.

Proudfit, Isabel, *James Fenimore Cooper*. New York: Julian Messner, 1946.
Ringe, Donald A., *James Fenimore Cooper*. Twayne's United States Authors Series. New York: Twayne Publishers, 1962.

William Cullen Bryant

William Cullen Bryant
/First Citizen of New York

During the mid-1870's, no weekday morning in New York City was complete without the appearance of William Cullen Bryant—white-haired, heavy-bearded, and in his eighties —trotting briskly along Fulton Street toward the new building which housed the offices of the New York *Evening Post*. Bryant had been editor-in-chief of the daily newspaper for over fifty years, and his routine in recent years had changed somewhat: He now arrived at 8:45 each morning, instead of 7:00. He no longer skipped lunch and worked on until four in the afternoon, when the *Post* went to press. Instead, he now left his office around noon, leaving last-minute administrative and editorial details to Parke Godwin, his son-in-law and associate editor of the paper. Bryant usually went on to one of the civic functions where his presence was ever in demand as first citizen of the city. His afternoon and evening hours were filled with giving speeches for every occasion, from ground-breakings, dedications, and the unveiling of statues to memorial addresses on the deaths of public figures.

Although Bryant's shoulders were now slightly stooped from years bent over an editor's desk and a scholar's notebook, he was still in robust health. He rose at 5:00 A.M. in summer and 5:30 in winter, and he never allowed a morning to pass without a period reserved for calisthenics. He still spurned the convenience of the newly installed elevator, and excelled in a light-footed pace up the successive flights of stairs to his comfortably furnished office on the ninth floor. At some period during the

morning he would take a break from the editorial he was labori-
ously piecing together (every word, every phrase carefully chosen) to chin himself on the frame of his office door.

Bryant was born in Cummington, Massachusetts, on November 3, 1794. His parents were Dr. Peter and Sarah Bryant. Less
than a year after Cullen was born, Dr. Bryant became involved
in a personal financial disaster. He had invested money in a
merchant ship. The cash he had used was borrowed. The investment failed and he was unable to repay the loan. To avoid being
thrown into debtors' prison, Dr. Bryant had to flee from Cummington. For several months he was afraid to even write a letter
to his wife for fear it would be intercepted by the police and his
whereabouts revealed. At last, on September 29, 1795, he wrote
to Sarah from Newport, Rhode Island:

Ah! my dear, if you knew what I have suffered since I saw you, by a
long illness, you would pity me—but such is my folly, I confess I
do not deserve it—I see my folly, and sincerely repent it & if I live
to return I shall put my affairs into such a train as to pay every man
his honest due—But I will not judge rashly—As for the vessel I
expected to be engaged in, I have heard nothing of it—My spirit
would not brook returning to you without anything—I have therefore
engaged surgeon on board a vessel from New York, for a voyage of
ten months, to sail round the Cape of Good Hope, to a Portuguese
settlement called Mozambique.

Dr. Bryant did not return to the United States until September, 1797. His financial hopes had not been realized, but the
family was joyful just to be together again. They settled in
Plainfield, Massachusetts, for a few months, and then moved the
short distance home to Cummington, where Dr. Bryant had reestablished his medical practice.

During Cullen's childhood the Republic of the United States
was still in its infancy. There were only fifteen states in the
Union, and most of the framers of the Constitution were still

politically active. Dr. Bryant was an ardent Federalist, and his two years away from the United States had not cooled his political interests. Nor was Sarah Bryant less positive in her political convictions, which paralleled those of her husband. It is not surprising, therefore, that Cullen, at the age of thirteen, became sharply aware of politics. In an autobiographical sketch written near the close of his life, he recalled his awakening to political affairs:

I read the newspapers of the Federal party, and took a strong interest in political questions. Under Mr. Jefferson's administration, in consequence of our disputes with Great Britain, an embargo was laid in 1807 upon all the ports of our republic, which, by putting a stop to all foreign commerce, had a disastrous effect upon many private interests, and embittered the hatred with which the Federalists regarded their political adversaries, and particularly Mr. Jefferson. I had written some satirical lines apostrophizing the President, which my father saw, and . . . encouraged me to write others in the same vein. This I did willingly, until the addition grew into a poem of several pages . . . .

Among other suggestions, the poem, which was entitled "The Embargo," hinted that Mr. Jefferson should "quit to abler hands, the helm of state . . . ." "The Embargo" so well expressed the sentiments of all loyal Federalists that Dr. Bryant took it to Boston and had it printed as a pamphlet, which appeared in 1808. Cullen's name was not on the title page; instead, "by a Youth of Thirteen" was imprinted there. The work sold quickly. The *Monthly Anthology*, a literary magazine, commented: "If this poem be really written by a youth of thirteen, it must be acknowledged an extraordinary performance. We have never met with a boy of that age who had attained to such a command of language and to so much poetic phraseology." Dr. Bryant published a second edition of the poem in 1809. This time Cullen's name did appear on the title page.

This was not the first time Cullen's work had appeared in

print for "public consumption." Three years earlier, when he was ten years old, a short poem of his had been printed in the *Hampshire Gazette*, published at North Hampton, a few miles from Cummington. By the time he was sixteen, Cullen had written thousands of lines of poetry which included elegies, odes, songs, and translations. Only some thirty of these poems remain in their entirety.

In reference to a poem he wrote when he was about fourteen, Bryant said, "My father read it, and told me that it was nothing but tinsel and would not do." Dr. Bryant was extremely demanding of his sons, all of whom possessed a marked ability to write poetry at an early age. Of his father's opinion of his verse, Bryant wrote, "There were only four lines among all that I had written which he would allow to be tolerable."

Cullen, like all the children in Cummington, received the first few years of his education from his parents. The town had no lower school. Thus he saw few people outside of immediate relatives and neighbors until he was sent away to prepare for college. Cummington was in the Berkshire Hills, an isolated section of New England. There was little social activity there other than corn huskings, apple parings, and "raisings" of timber frames for houses and barns. Almost everything necessary for daily life was manufactured in the home, or grown on the farm. Cullen wore nothing except the garments made by his mother from cloth she had woven. There was nothing in his surroundings to disturb the natural development of his mind and character.

As his childhood unfolded, he was deeply influenced by the quiet woodlands and the gentle Berkshire slopes that surrounded his family home; when he entered his teen years his thoughts and spiritual reflections rested on "uncertain shapes that cheat the sight," to quote his poem, "The Journey of Life." In later years he wrote:

I cannot say . . . that I found my boyhood the happiest part of my life. I had more frequent ailments than afterward, my hopes were more feverish and impatient, and my disappointments were more acute. The restraints on my liberty of action . . . were irksome, and felt as fetters, that galled my spirit and gave it pain.

When Cullen was sixteen, he was enrolled in Williams College at Williamstown, Massachusetts. Both he and his father would have preferred that he go to Harvard University, where the academic atmosphere would have been more conducive to his literary yearnings. But Dr. Bryant, with three younger sons still to be educated, was forced to choose a more modest school for Cullen, his oldest.

Of his college career Cullen wrote: "My stay in college was hardly long enough to form those close and life-long intimacies of which college life is generally the parent. . . ." "Where the number of teachers was so small [there were only four faculty members], it could hardly be expected that the course of studies should be very extensive . . . ." Bryant's single memorial to Williams College was a brief, acid poem written during his student days:

> Why should I sing those reverend domes,
>   Where Science rests in grave repose?
> Ah me! their terrors and their glooms
>   Only the wretched inmate knows. . . .

Cullen left Williams College in May, 1811, seven months after he had enrolled. The possibility of his going on to Yale the following fall had been discussed, but his father proved unable to send him because of the tuition costs there. Thus ended Cullen's academic education. He later regretted his haste in leaving Williams College since he might have been able to complete his college education had he remained there.

Since there were no funds for further pursuit of the liberal arts, Cullen was faced with the necessity of choosing a profession. He had no talent for the ministry and was not interested in farming or following his father into medicine. The law offered more opportunity for a young man of Cullen's nature and talent than either the ministry or medicine, the only other fields open to him besides farming. In December, 1811, he settled in Worthington, Massachusetts, where he began to read law in the office of an attorney, Samuel Howe, a friend of Dr. Bryant's. Cullen carried on his studies faithfully, but he found his mind constantly pulled back to literature. There was always a novel or book of poetry hidden among the papers on his desk, from which he surreptitiously read a few lines during the long days spent poring over legal books and documents. A few moments alone with Donne, Spenser, or Cowper was almost as refreshing as a walk in his beloved Berkshire Hills.

But the well-intentioned Mr. Howe discouraged his interest in literature. Howe noticed Cullen's surreptitious reading habits, usually indulged during his lunch period, and his occasional scribbling of verse. In an effort to give his student the best of advice, he told Cullen not to waste time on a pursuit so unrewarding, but to devote every waking moment to the study of law. In a sincere desire to please Mr. Howe, Cullen put aside his books. This left him with only one interest outside the study of law: his delight in botany, which often took him on long hikes through the woods around Worthington. But even his pleasure in collecting plants and other specimens did not relieve his feelings of frustration and sadness over his future career. It was not surprising that the surrounding hills, brooks, trees, and streams and the changing seasons should all begin to take on a symbolism of life and death to Cullen.

About this time an epidemic of typhus broke out in Worthington. Many of Cullen's friends died from the disease. Among them was the bride of a close friend. This loss was very close to Cullen's heart, and he could no longer ignore the persistent urge to express his feelings in verse. At the request of the young woman's husband, he wrote a poem in her memory. It began with these lines:

Alas! When late for thee I twined,
    And thy lost love, the bridal wreath,
I little thought so soon to bind
    The cypress round the urn of death.

Cullen's life seemed shrouded by death. His father was suffering from what was to prove a fatal disease, and he himself was not well. Less than a month after the death of his friend's wife he received notice that his maternal grandfather had died. He had grown up with Grandfather Snell always nearby, so this, too, was a deep loss for Cullen and added to his morbid reflections about life and what appeared to be its inevitable end, death.

Well out of attorney Howe's sight, Cullen embarked on an intensive reading of the "graveyard poets," English writers of the eighteenth century who took death as the theme for their verse. The mood of their poetry fitted Cullen's depressed state of mind.

Occasionally Cullen's thoughts were diverted from the topic of death to the beauty of nature, as when he addressed "The Yellow Violet":

When beechen buds begin to swell,
    And woods the blue-bird's warble know,
The yellow violet's modest bell
    Peeps from the last year's leaves below.

Cullen's intellectual development was taking a marked direction toward the time when he would compose the first draft of the poem which would be perhaps his greatest achievement in verse: "Thanatopsis." This was the first truly classic poem to be written in America.

Obedient as Cullen wished to be in the course of study planned for him by his father, he was far from happy at the thought of following a legal career. He wished now that he had not been so hasty in throwing up his opportunity for a college education; even Williams College, with its unimaginative curriculum, would have been better than the stuffy law office in Worthington, which he described as "consisting of a blacksmith-shop and a cow-stable, at either of which places he might be found . . . ."

In 1814, after two and a half years of study in Mr. Howe's law office in Worthington, Cullen moved to Bridgewater, Massachusetts. Here he continued his study in the law office of William Baylies, a well-known attorney and member of the United States Congress. Bridgewater was an improvement over Worthington. It was a larger town and offered a broader range of interests for Cullen, including the well-stocked library of his grandfather, Dr. Phillip Bryant, one of the town's most respected citizens.

Although Bridgewater did not provide the complete answer to Cullen's dreams of a broader intellectual horizon, life there was much less lonely for him. He lived with his grandparents and again enjoyed the pleasures of family life. Grandfather Bryant was proud of Cullen's literary talent and encouraged him to pursue it, along with his law study. Cullen wrote a friend, "I am certainly as well contented with this place as I could be with any, and I would not exchange it for Worthington if the wealth of the Indies were thrown into that side of the balance."

But in spite of Cullen's determination to be an obedient son and make the best of law study, he still yearned for more extensive literary opportunities. In vain he wrote to his father, pleading to be allowed to locate in a Boston law firm. Dr. Bryant's reply was adamant: "You have cost me already four hundred dollars at Mr. Howe's, and I have other children equally entitled to my care." This particular letter contained even more sobering news. "My health is imperfect," Dr. Bryant continued, "I have suffered much from the fatigues of the last season, and, as I may not long be with you, I must do what I can for you all while I am still here."

The news was a shock to Cullen and awakened him from his self-centered musings. He turned his mind more seriously than ever to the law and did not again waver in his determination to complete his work and join the Massachusetts bar.

The social and cultural life of Bridgewater was a novelty to Cullen. There were more people with whom he found interests in common, and Grandfather Bryant wasted no time in letting it be known to friends and neighbors that his grandson was the composer of "The Embargo," still popular among Federalists, although six years had gone by since it first appeared in print.

A month after Cullen arrived in Bridgewater he was invited to compose a Fourth of July ode. Next to Christmas, Independence Day was the most important holiday celebration in any New England town. Cullen's ode rejoiced in the defeat of Napoleon in France, and in spite of the war between America and England then being fought, glorified England's victory over France. All reference to the War of 1812 was conspicuously absent. This was in keeping with the intellectual climate of Bridgewater, whose citizens were ardent Federalists and, like Cullen, considered the war "Mr. Madison's War"—not a Federalist affair.

The War of 1812 had disastrous effects on the youthful country as a whole, but New England experienced greater financial damage than any other section of the United States. Not only had taxes skyrocketed, but New England's shipping industry was at a standstill. Trade with England had stopped, and American merchant ships, most of them out of New England ports, were at the mercy of British warships wherever they ventured.

The citizens of New England had by 1814 reached the peak of frustration and indignation. They had not started the war; they bore no grudge against England. They declared their intent to secede from the Union and proceeded with the task of raising an army. It was their plan to throw off the "yoke" of the Madison administration and form an independent nation composed of the New England states.

Cullen, who was normally a level-headed young man, was caught up in this mass hysteria and applied for a commission in the militia. He wrote a friend: "Yesterday we received orders from the Major General of this division to detach eight hundred and ninety men from this brigade to march to the defence of Plymouth. This takes all the militia from this quarter. They marched this morning. The streets were full of them a little while ago, but now the place is as solitary and silent as a desert."

In November, 1814, Cullen became seriously ill and was forced to leave his law study for a few weeks. He went home to Cummington for a rest. With his father already in poor health, and Cullen suspected of having the early symptoms of tuberculosis, the atmosphere at home was depressing. Cullen's morbid state of mind, with which he had been struggling since his early days at Worthington, was intensified. Again he seemed overwhelmed by a consciousness of death.

In spite of the cheerless circumstances at home, Cullen regained his health rapidly. He was back in Bridgewater by December 20. Shortly thereafter he received his commission in the militia. But it came too late for him to take part in this prelude to rebellion; the Treaty of Ghent was signed December 24, 1814, although news of the agreement did not reach America until February, 1815. The battle of New Orleans had taken place in January, two weeks after the war had officially ended.

Bryant passed his bar examination in August, 1815. He then returned to Cummington for about three months. He could not enter the practice of law immediately because he would not reach the legal age of twenty-one until his birthday, November 3, 1815. It is possible that during this stay at home Cullen wrote the first draft of his poem "Thanatopsis." Several Bryant scholars have concluded that he wrote this draft sometime in 1815. The part of the poem which he first committed to paper was only a fragment of the poem he evidently planned to complete at a later date. It was Bryant's practice to compose an early draft of a poem and then work on it until he felt it was complete. Bryant began this incomplete poem of forty-nine lines in the middle of a line:

> Yet a few days, and thee
> The all-beholding sun shall see no more
> In all his course; nor yet in the cold ground,
> Where thy pale form was laid, with many tears,
> Nor in the embrace of ocean, shall exist
> Thy image.

He ended the fragment as abruptly as he had begun it, in the middle of a line. He also left it untitled. "Thanatopsis," as it would eventually be named, did not appear in its final form until 1821, when *Poems*, the first volume of his collected verse, was published. This was six years after he had written the first draft. Just before *Poems* went to press in 1821, he added new lines for both a beginning and an ending. The powerful opening lines now read:

> To him who in the love of Nature holds
> Communion with her visible forms, she speaks
> A various language . . . .

The poem ends with an injunction to go to the grave not "like the quarry-slave at night,/ Scourged to his dungeon" but with "an unfaltering trust."

After spending several months with his family, Bryant opened his first law office in December, 1815, in Plainfield, a small village seven miles from Cummington. It may have been during one of his walks to and from Plainfield that lines for his poem "To a Waterfowl" took form. The fourth stanza of this poem, written in 1815, suggests the young lawyer's hesitant but hopeful outlook for his future:

> There is a Power whose care
> Teaches thy way along that pathless coast—
> The desert and illimitable air—
> Lone wandering, but not lost.

Six months later he was invited to enter a partnership with a young lawyer in Great Barrington, Massachusetts. Bryant was delighted at the prospect of moving to a larger town and broadening not only his law practice but also the scope of his intellectual and social interests. He had more than average hopes for success in the practice of law and planned to continue his writing. But as the months slipped rapidly by, his practice expanded more quickly than he had expected. Since every waking moment was given to keeping up with his practice and his competitors, he would have to face a decision, and soon, as to whether he should continue to dabble in literature or put the subject out of his mind and concentrate on the law.

Cullen did not yet know it, but his cherished dream of a literary career was soon to be realized. An old friend of Dr. Bryant's, Willard Phillips, was a member of the editorial board of *The North American Review*, a new literary magazine being published in Boston. Dr. Bryant had partially recovered from his illness and was now well enough to serve in the state legislature, which met in Boston. Shortly after he arrived there he wrote Cullen that he had been in contact with Phillips, who desired that Cullen contribute something to his new review. "Prose or poetry will be equally acceptable. I wish," Dr. Bryant continued, "if you have leisure, you would comply, as it might be the means of introducing you to notice in the capital [of Massachusetts]. Those who contribute are generally known to the *literati* in and about Boston."

By this time Cullen had decided that his life would be devoted to a legal career and stubbornly resisted the return to poetry. But Dr. Bryant was not discouraged by his son's refusal to comply with Phillips' request for a contribution. Searching some papers that Cullen had left in a desk at home, he found several incomplete pieces of poetry, including the one later to become famous as "Thanatopsis." Although he was well aware of Cullen's practice of reworking everything he wrote, Dr. Bryant copied these verses on fresh paper and took them to Boston without consulting Cullen about his feelings in the matter. Once he arrived in Boston, Dr. Bryant went to deliver the packet of poetry to Phillips' home. Finding that Phillips was away, Bryant left the packet, with his card attached to the poems. Since the poems were unsigned and in Dr. Bryant's handwriting, Phillips assumed that they were his own work. Delighted with what he thought were contributions from his friend, he took the manuscript to his fellow editors across the river in Cambridge: Edward T. Channing and Richard Henry Dana, Sr. Both listened attentively while he read the poems aloud. At the end of the reading, Dana remarked with a smile: "Phillips, you have been imposed upon; no one on this side of the Atlantic is capable of writing such verses."

Phillips answered confidently: "I know the gentleman who wrote . . . them . . . very well; an old acquaintance of mine—Dr. Bryant—at this moment sitting in the State-House in Boston as Senator from Hampshire County."

"Then," replied Dana, "I must have a look at him."

"Arrived at the senate," Dana later reported, "I caused the doctor to be pointed out to me. I looked at him with profound attention and interest; and, while I saw a man of striking presence, the stamp of genius seemed to me to be wanting. It is a good head, I said to myself, but I do not see 'Thanatopsis' in it." Dana returned to Cambridge somewhat disappointed.

Dr. Bryant, proud father that he was, wasted no time in correcting the mistake concerning the author of "Thanatopsis." "I have . . . set him right on that subject," Dr. Bryant later wrote Cullen.

Since the several pieces of poetry which Dr. Bryant gave to Phillips were untitled, the editors assumed each to be a separate poem. But since the texts in two pieces were similar, they were printed side by side under a single title, "Thanatopsis." The editor who prepared the material was a Greek scholar and selected the title because both poems dealt with death. "Thana-topsis" is derived from *thanatos*, the word for death in Greek. Another untitled piece was labeled "A Fragment" and published along with "Thanatopsis" in the September, 1817, edition of *The North American Review*.

At the time of its publication, "Thanatopsis" did not attract much attention outside the intellectual circle who subscribed to *The North American Review*, but it was acknowledged as the first piece of lyric poetry to have bridged the creative gap be-tween English and American poetry and was judged the first truly original poem ever produced in America.

Bryant was a lyric poet, one of the first in America to recognize that the simple beauty of nature was suitable material for poet-ry. During his lifetime he produced seven volumes of poetry. As each volume appeared, he added new poems and revised some of his earlier works to appeal to the generation which had grown to maturity since the first publication of *Poems*. He also translated *The Iliad* and *The Odyssey* into English.

Bryant's pleas for a purely American literature prepared the way for Ralph Waldo Emerson, who was destined to make the final declaration of American literary independence from Eu-rope. In an article for *The North American Review*, Bryant laid bare the American writer's penchant for copying the style and content of English and European literature:

... tinged with a sickly and affected imitation of the peculiar man-ner of some of the late popular poets of England. We speak not of a disposition to emulate whatever is beautiful and excellent in their writings ... but we desire to set a mark on that servile habit of copying, which adopts the vocabulary of some favourite author, and apes the fashion of his sentences, and cramps and forces the ideas into a shape, which they would not naturally have taken ....

His new-found success, though relatively small, stirred Bry-ant's old desire to leave village life for the more stimulating atmosphere of a big city, preferably Boston. Dr. Bryant wisely suggested to his son: "But will it not be better for you to continue where you are a few years, and lay a solid foundation, while you have your time to yourself without interruption? I, however, do not wish to influence your determination in respect to the disposition of your own affairs. Every young man who intends to make his way in the world . . . must rely at last upon his own talent and exertions."

When his father died not long afterwards, Bryant again resigned himself to the fact that the law practice must be placed first in his affairs. It was necessary to send money home to help support his mother. At the peak of his earning powers as a lawyer, his income never went over five hundred dollars a year. All of his cases were civil affairs, mainly involving the payment of debts. Most of his clients were of the laboring class, with whom he found little in common outside the courtroom. It was natural that the young lawyer should snatch at any straw that might offer escape to a career and surroundings more congenial to his interests.

It was a partial relief to his frustrations when Bryant met a Miss Fanny Fairchild, in the spring following his father's death. Fanny was a small, dainty, and very pretty blonde. She possessed just enough modesty to be appealing to Bryant's poetic turn of mind, but enough wit, wisdom, and charm to arouse his masculine interest. Her step was "as the wind, that weaves/ Its playful way among the leaves," as he wrote in his poem, "Oh, Fairest of the Rural Maids." She enjoyed good books, especially books of poetry, and had read his poem "Thanatopsis." It was not long before he asked her to be his wife. They were married on June 11, 1821.

Cullen and Fanny began their life together in two rooms, sharing a kitchen with other lodgers. For these modest accommodations they paid the sum of thirty dollars a year.

The marriage was to prove an unusually happy one. At Fanny's death, almost half a century later, Bryant wrote to one of his brothers: "We have been married more than forty-five years, and all my plans, even to the least important, were laid with some reference to her judgment or her pleasure." Bryant survived her by twelve years.

In August, 1821, Bryant delivered the Phi Beta Kappa address at the Harvard commencement. Entitled "The Ages," the address was in verse form. This was the most important step thus far in the development of his literary career, for it led to the publication of his first book of poems.

The audience to which Bryant spoke was distinguished, "a formidable one for a young man to front," reported one spectator. Miss Eliza Quincy, another spectator, recorded that his "appearance was pleasing, refined, and intellectual; his manner was calm and dignified . . . . [The poem] excited more repeated tributes of applause than could have been anticipated . . . ."

Bryant had barely finished delivering his address and stepped from the platform when Dana and Phillips rushed up to him with the proposal that his collected verse, including "The Ages," be published. Bryant was unconvinced that he was ready to allow the publication of a volume composed entirely of his own work, but he was overruled by his two enthusiastic friends. In the autumn, *Poems, by William Cullen Bryant* was published. It was a forty-four page pamphlet with paper covers and contained ten selections, including, besides "The Ages," "The Yellow Violet" and "Thanatopsis."

About this time a New York lawyer and friend of Bryant's named Henry D. Sedgewick saw a play Bryant had written. *The Heroes*, staged in Great Barrington, was not a success, yet Sedgewick saw in it Bryant's potential as a writer for magazines. He urged Bryant to come to New York and embark upon a full-time writing career.

New York City was not the Boston of Bryant's dreams, but he made numerous trips to the city and at last obtained a post as coeditor of the *New York Review and Athenaeum Magazine*. It paid one thousand dollars a year, a comfortable income for that time, and twice what he was earning from his law practice. He was already being paid two hundred dollars a year by the *United States Literary Gazette* to write one hundred lines of verse a month. It was clear to Bryant that his potential income in the field of publications was much higher than in law. He sold his practice without further hesitation, and settled Fanny and his young daughter Frances with his family until he could make suitable living arrangements for them in the city. (A second daughter, Julia, was born several years later.)

Bryant's exceptional and intimate knowledge of poetry soon became known throughout New York's intellectual circles. In the autumn of 1825 he was invited by the Athenaeum Society to deliver a series of lectures on poetry. These lectures proved to be so popular the series continued for five years, and Bryant was appointed a professor in the newly founded National Academy of Arts.

Meanwhile, the *Review* did not do well and merged with another periodical a year after Bryant became coeditor. Although Bryant was given a quarter interest in the publication, his salary was reduced to five hundred dollars a year. For a brief period he entered law practice in New York City; at least his family would be fed and have a roof over its head.

Bryant sat in his office one morning in June, 1826, reflecting on his problems: the *Review* had failed, and he had been forced to return to the drudgery of law practice; had he made a mistake in moving his family to New York City, in giving up his practice in Great Barrington for what now appeared an unsure future in journalism and the world of letters? Should he remain in law, since it had been forced on him again, and not take any more chances? He had responsibilities for two other lives besides his own. His family must come first. What should he do; in which direction should he turn?

As these thoughts distracted Bryant from the dull legal affairs at hand, a young man appeared at his office door. He was the son of William Coleman, editor of the New York *Evening Post*. Young Coleman told Bryant that his father had been in a serious accident and would be unable to return to his editorial duties for many months. Bryant was asked if he would accept a temporary position as editor of the *Post*.

Bryant was astonished at the sudden offer; the New York *Evening Post*, founded by William Coleman with the backing of Alexander Hamilton and other Federalists in 1801, was one of the most respected and influential daily newspapers in the city. He needed time to think; he suddenly felt very unsure of himself. He told the young man he would come to the *Post*'s office in an hour to deliver his decision.

An hour later he walked into the newspaper office and accepted the position. He found an unused desk in a corner, settled down to work, and began what was to be a career with the New York *Evening Post* spanning more than half a century. This was in July, 1826. His official title was associate editor, and he bought a small share of the newspaper.

In a letter to Henry Dana he described his new position: "I am a small proprietor in the establishment, and am a gainer by the arrangement. It will afford me a comfortable livelihood after I have paid for the *eighth part*, which is the amount of my share. I do not like politics . . . but . . . politics and a belly-full are better than poetry and starvation."

Bryant's position as editor-in-chief of the New York *Evening Post* was made official three years later, after the death of William Coleman in 1829. Bryant acquired additional financial interest in the *Post* and eventually became the major stockholder. He brought to the editorship a culture which American journalism had not known before. His readers quickly learned to expect his editorials to open with a suitable quotation from the Greek classics, or a story from the legal lore he had mastered at the bar, or an apt quotation from English poetry. He knew the power of the press and resolved that in his hands it would not fall short of the noblest ideals. According to one historian, his "power as an editor lay simply in his soundness of judgment, and his unwavering courage in maintaining it."

Bryant wrote that journalism could be endangered by "the strong temptation which it sets before men, to betray the cause of truth to public opinion, and to fall in with what are supposed to be the views held by a contemporaneous majority, which are sometimes perfectly right and sometimes grossly wrong." From the outset of his editorial career, Bryant came into sharp conflict with public opinion. He insisted upon the rights of the individual but maintained that the individual possessed certain duties toward his fellow man. Bryant, the poet, had evolved into the journalist of sound judgment and common sense. His associate on the *Post* and future son-in-law, Parke Godwin, first met him in 1832. Godwin left this graphic description of Bryant's physical appearance at that time:

He was of middle age and medium height, spare in figure, with a clean-shaven face, unusually large head, bright eyes, and a wearied, severe, almost saturnine expression of countenance. One, however, remarked at once the exceeding gentleness of his manner, and a rare sweetness in the tone of his voice, as well as an extraordinary purity in his selection and pronunciation of English. His conversation was easy, but not fluent, and he had a habit of looking the person he addressed so directly in the eyes that it was not a little embarrassing at first. A certain air of abstractedness in his face made you set him down as a scholar whose thoughts were wandering away to his books; and yet the deep lines about the mouth told of struggle either with himself or with the world.

Bryant did not grow his famous beard until 1853, during a trip to Europe.

In February, 1843, he wrote his brother Austin: "Congratulate me! ... I have made a bargain for about forty acres of solid earth at Hempstead Harbor, on the north side of Long Island. . . ." There was an old mansion on the estate, surrounded by land and trees. Fresh-water lakes were on the property and there was a good view of the harbor. Bryant named his estate Cedarmere because of the abundance of cedar trees on the property.

Bryant had grown in wealth far beyond any of his earlier expectations. Yet he still lived simply, preferring to walk rather than be driven in a carriage and choosing oatmeal over any available delicacy. His most lavish entertainment was to have a well-loved friend spend a weekend at Cedarmere. Besides Cedarmere, the chief outward signs of his wealth were his red-brick town house on Carmine Street in Greenwich Village and his ancestral home at Cummington, which he had acquired out of sentiment. In later years he moved his town residence to 24 West Fifteenth Street, New York City.

As the editor of a leading daily newspaper in New York City, Bryant became increasingly interested in politics. When the Free Soil Party became active, he was immediately drawn to it because of its firm stand against the spread of slavery and supported it editorially in the *Post*. But when the Free Soilers pushed the Fugitive Slave Act through Congress in 1850, he became disenchanted with the party because this act was a compromise with the slaveholding states. In the presidential election of 1852 he gave editorial support to Franklin Pierce, who was nominated by the Democratic Party. By the time the 1856 presidential election came up, the Republican Party had been formed from the stronger antislavery remnants of the Whig and Free Soil parties. Bryant placed his editorial powers in support of the new party because of its demand for the total abolition of slavery throughout the United States.

When the Republican Party chose Abraham Lincoln as its presidential candidate, Bryant rallied the newspaper editors of New York to the support of this leading opponent of slavery. But when Lincoln failed to show the leadership expected of him after the Civil War began in 1861, Bryant was also among the first to become impatient with the President. New York editors began writing editorials which condemned Lincoln's weakness as commander-in-chief and demanded more positive statements from him concerning the objectives of the war. The public, too, grew disillusioned with Lincoln's lack of action and his vague attitude toward the slavery issue.

At last it was decided that a member of the press should be sent to the White House to see Lincoln. Bryant was chosen because of his tact and wise use of words. His assignment: to ask Lincoln for a positive statement on the moral issue involved in the War Between the States.

Bryant's interview with Lincoln appeared unrewarding. The President gave generously of his time to the Editor and was cordial, but he had very little to say. Bryant left the capital somewhat frustrated over what appeared to be a lack of response from the Chief Executive. Weeks passed, and still there was no positive statement from the White House on the aims of the war. Bryant then began an editorial barrage calculated to expose "the weakness and vacillation of the Administration." At last Lincoln and his Cabinet began to formulate a new policy toward the war and its objectives. On September 22, 1862, the Emancipation Proclamation was made public. It became effective on January 1, 1863.

Bryant was one of the few northern editors to question the militant attitude the Republican Party continued to hold toward the South after the end of the Civil War. The military occupation of the southern states by federal troops during the Reconstruction period was called "protectionism." But it was actually an expression of contempt felt by the postwar Republican administration for the defeated enemy. Bryant's deep concern was for the reunification of the nation. He felt only scorn for the carpetbaggers, scalawags, and politicians such as Thaddeus Stevens, who were taking every opportunity to humiliate the South and its people.

In spite of his qualms about Republican policies toward the

South during this critical period, Bryant had even less hope that a change of parties would ease conditions in the South. Therefore, when the presidential campaign of 1872 was launched, Bryant placed the *Post*'s support behind Grant. He considered Grant weak and ineffectual but less of a threat to the country as a whole than the flamboyant Horace Greeley, editor and founder of the *New York Tribune* and Democratic nominee for President. Bryant, who considered Greeley to be erratic, eccentric, crude, and boyish, argued in an editorial that a candidate for the office of President of the United States "should be, at least, a gentleman!"

The *Post* moved to a new building in 1875, but Bryant seldom occupied his handsome new office. He preferred a chair and desk in a corner of the composing room, where he was free from boring callers. Though he was essentially compassionate by nature, he could be blunt on occasion and felt no hesitancy in offending those whom he disliked. He grew testy in later years and was especially sensitive to suggestions that he was losing his physical vigor.

Bryant's production of poetry decreased as he grew older, but his influence as a vigorous and liberal editor made him one of the most dynamic figures of the nineteenth century. In 1872 hs was mentioned as a presidential possibility, but he considered journalism a jealous mistress and declined all offers of public office.

To give a proper assessment of Bryant's accomplishments, it is necessary to divide his life into three parts. The first part involved his early life as a young lawyer and poet. He received early recognition of his poetic genius and originality through his poem "Thanatopsis." The delivery of his poem "The Ages" at the 1821 Harvard College Commencement marked his recognition by the American intellectual community as the foremost poet of the period.

The second part of Bryant's life was dedicated to the development of the *Evening Post* into a great daily newspaper. This endeavor demanded the whole of Bryant's thought. It called upon him to lay aside the abstract musings of a poet and face a very real world wherein the joys and sorrows of mankind and the course of the nation's daily affairs remolded him into a man of the hour. It would have been impossible to think of the retiring young lawyer and poet from Great Barrington, as he was upon his arrival in New York City in 1825, as the self-confident editor who called upon President Lincoln in 1862. This was Bryant, the public figure, the man willing to criticize the President of the United States in print, the personal representative of the New York press to the White House.

The third part of Bryant's career was an outgrowth of the second part, because as the editor of New York City's leading evening newspaper he could not avoid becoming involved with the growth and progress of the city. Bryant's civic interests were widespread. They ranged from his defense of the striking journeyman tailors of New York in 1836 to a prominent role in welcoming Charles Dickens to the city in 1842; from a role in the founding of the Republican Party in 1854 to an enthusiastic support of Central Park. Until two weeks before his death on June 12, 1878, no public occasion, such as the dedication of a new park or statue or a memorial service for an honored citizen, was complete without a poem or an address by William Cullen Bryant.

An associate on the *Evening Post* recalled that in Bryant's later years, whether he wrote an editorial or not, he read carefully and corrected all the daily proofs. "He would pass through the editorial rooms with a cheery good morning; he would sit down by one's desk and talk if there was aught to talk about; or, if asked a question while passing, would stand while answering it, and frequently would relate some anecdote suggested by the question or offer some apt quotation."

Bryant, who came to New York City when pigs still ran through the streets and Greenwich Village was a summer resort for city dwellers, lived into the flamboyant Gilded Age of the 1870's. Born four years after the death of Benjamin Franklin, he lived to see Edison begin his experiments in electricity and Bell's "far-speaker" give threat to the messenger boy.

One of the numerous memorial tributes to Bryant summed up his multifaceted life and career:

A patriarch of our literature, and in a permanent sense the oldest of our poets, a scholar familiar with many languages and literatures, finely sensitive to the influence of nature, and familiar with trees and birds and flowers, he was especially fitted, it might be thought, for scholarly seclusion and the delights of the strict literary life. But . . . the poet became distinctively an American and a public political leader. . . . His lofty personality rose above the clamor of selfish ambition, and in his life he reconciled, both in fact and to the popular imagination, the seeming incompatibility of literary taste and accomplishment and superiority with constant political activity.

Suggested Reading*

BRYANT ANTHOLOGIES:

Poems of William Cullen Bryant, The. Edited by Louis Untermeyer. New York: The Limited Editions Club, 1947.

Poetical Works of William Cullen Bryant, The. Edited by Parke Godwin. 2 vols. New York: Russell & Russell, reprint, 1967.

Prose Writings of William Cullen Bryant, The. Edited by Parke Godwin. 2 vols. New York: Russell & Russell, reprint, 1964.

William Cullen Bryant: Selections from his Poetry and Prose. Edited by Samuel Sillen. New York: International Publishers, 1945.

BOOKS ABOUT BRYANT:

Berbrich, Joan D., *Three Voices of Paumanok.* Port Washington: Kennikat Press, 1969.

Brown, Charles H., *Bryant.* New York: Charles Scribner's Sons, 1971.

Godwin, Parke, *A Biography of William Cullen Bryant, with Extracts from His Private Correspondence.* 2 vols. New York: Russell & Russell, reprint, 1967.

McLean, Albert F., *William Cullen Bryant.* Twayne's United States Authors Series. New York: Twayne Publishers, 1964.

Peckham, Harry H., *Gotham Yankee: A Biography of William Cullen Bryant.* New York: Russell & Russell, 1971.

* The author has listed popular editions for convenient reference.

Edgar Allan Poe

Edgar Allan Poe
/ A Dreamer within a Dream

"In Edgar Poe the man and the writer are united by so many and so close bonds," wrote a French literary critic in 1865, "the genius of the one shows so much the deeds and exploits of the other, that it is folly to consider them in any other way than in relation to each other."

Poe was understood as a man and as a writer by French and English men of letters long before American writers appreciated his creative genius. A few American literary men, such as the novelist John Pendleton Kennedy and Thomas W. White, publisher of the *Southern Literary Messenger*, freely acknowledged his genius and were his friends and benefactors. "But in any society," an American biographer has written, "Poe would have been an outcast." One of the reasons for this was what appeared to be his compulsive drive toward self-destruction. The periods in Poe's life when his literary career seemed to be moving smoothly were disrupted by his desire for drugs or alcohol, or by a sudden whim to move on to what he thought would be a more productive literary center of the country.

Yet there were also outside pressures which further aggravated his personal problems. Poe lived in a society that was too involved in its own robust and rapid expansion to understand a complex and sensitive nature like his. The works of James Fenimore Cooper and Washington Irving are good examples of the literary flavor of the times. They were fresh yet traditional in subject matter; books which everyone in the family read and enjoyed. Poe, in contrast, dealt with the dark and mysterious.

91

His was a literary form and flavor totally new and unfamiliar to American writers and readers. It is true that the reading public at that time was enthralled with the gloomy shades of the Gothic novel and found in Poe's tales an intensification of this mood. Yet American writers as a whole were unimpressed by his strange genius. He did not have the good fortune to receive even the grudging reception from fellow writers that the rebel Whitman received from Emerson. James Russell Lowell summed up this attitude toward Poe:

There comes Poe with his raven, like Barnaby Rudge,
Three-fifths of him genius and two-fifths sheer fudge . . . .

Much of the blame for this lack of respect from other writers lies with Poe himself. It was brought about by his sharp and often unfair criticism of their work, inspired by his envy of their good fortune. But the fact remains that Poe was an innovator in American literature. He defined and refined the short story. In his more than sixty short stories he illustrated the rule of sacrificing every unnecessary element of the narrative for the final effect. One of the best examples of this is found in "The Black Cat." Not until the last paragraph does the reader find "the hideous beast whose craft had seduced" the narrator to murder and then led him to the hangman's noose.

Tragedy stalked Poe's life, beginning with the death of his mother when he was not quite three. Elizabeth Poe and her husband David were both actors—members of a profession considered not completely respectable in the early nineteenth century. Edgar, their second child, was born January 19, 1809, in Boston, Massachusetts, where their troupe was playing. The Poes had an older son, William Henry Leonard, born in 1807, who had been left with his paternal grandparents in Baltimore shortly after his birth. Elizabeth and David were too poor and their lives too transient to keep him with them.

In September, 1809, the Poes arrived in New York City, where they played at the Park Theatre. David Poe disappeared on July 4, 1810. He was assumed dead, although it is not actually known whether he deserted his family and lived on or died and was buried in an unmarked grave in Potter's Field.

Elizabeth, who was expecting another child, rejoined the Virginia Players, where she had been a member before her marriage. While she was playing in Norfolk, Rosalie was born. It was the practice at that time for an actress who was expecting a baby to remain active on the stage until the birth of the child, often until the day of its arrival. Soon after Rosalie was born, Elizabeth reappeared on the stage. Despite failing health, she struggled on for almost a year, until she arrived in Richmond, where she became too ill to continue. Her career as an actress was at an end.

In the gray light of the shortening days of late fall, Elizabeth Poe lay dying in a cold, shabbily furnished room. Newspaper items about her tragic situation drew many visitors to the dingy dwelling. Among the ladies who called with gifts of food and sickroom supplies was Frances Allan, wife of a Richmond merchant, John Allan. Frances, who had been unable to bear any children during her eight years of marriage, could not help being moved by the dying mother and her children.

On the morning after Elizabeth Poe died, Frances Allan and a friend, Mrs. William MacKensie, came for the children. Mrs. MacKensie took Rosalie, and Frances took Edgar. The young boy's only inheritance was a miniature portrait of his mother, a bundle of letters, a purse with a few locks of his mother's and father's hair, and a painting by her of Boston Harbor, on the back of which she had written a message charging him to "love Boston, the place of his birth, and where his mother found her best and most sympathetic friends."

His mother's death meant little more to young Edgar than a change of circumstances and surroundings. The presence of a woman he had called "mama" was suddenly gone; but replacing her was another woman who was possibly even more affectionate. Yet Edgar became increasingly aware of an elusive sorrow, a sense of gloom hanging over his life; and these emotions surfaced again and again in his work.

His sister Rosalie remained with the MacKensies until the Civil War, when the family was broken up and scattered. Rosalie saw her brother Edgar daily throughout their childhood, and again when he returned to Richmond to become editor of the *Southern Literary Messenger*. Rosalie never developed mentally much beyond the age of fourteen. It was her retarded mental growth that in later years was to add to Edgar's concern over his own mental insecurity. When Poe was in Richmond courting his beloved Elmira, shortly before his tragic end, Rosalie was his constant companion. She died in 1874 at a charitable institution in Washington, D.C.

Edgar was soon settled in the Allan household. John Allan at first assumed that the arrangement would be temporary, but it was not long before it became apparent that it was likely to be permanent. Allan was thrifty and demanding, though not harsh. He had come to Virginia from Scotland in 1795 to work for his uncle, William Galt, a wealthy Richmond merchant. He was not a handsome man—he has been described as having a large curved nose and small piercing eyes. But he was energetic and ambitious. In 1800 he and Charles Ellis, who had also worked for Galt, established their own business, which was a thriving enterprise by the time Edgar appeared on the scene.

The Allan household was located in an apartment over the firm of Ellis and Allan. It was the custom at that time for merchants to live over their places of business. Mrs. Allan's sister, Miss Nancy Valentine, lived with the Allans. Although Allan's business was flourishing by 1811, he did not feel that he could afford the addition of Edgar. He still had hopes that he and his wife would have children of their own. He was sending money to Scotland to help his widowed sisters and their children. He was the father of illegitimate children by two women in Richmond and was contributing to their support. All these expenses were creating a strain on his budget. Besides, what did he know of this offspring of an obscure actor and actress, whose social standing was not of the highest order?

Frances was unaware of her husband's escapades with the other women and remained oblivious of the situation until shortly before her death. That is why Allan did not explain to her his entire objection to taking Edgar into his home permanently.

She, of course, knew of the necessity of supporting his sisters' children and could be easily reasoned with from this basis—or so John Allan thought. He would let her have her way for a little while, until he could make other arrangements for the boy.

But an unforeseen tragedy which occurred shortly after Elizabeth Poe's death was to make a drastic change in John Allan's planning. During a gala Christmas celebration the Richmond Theatre burned to the ground. Seventy-three of Richmond's most prominent citizens died in the fire. There were many orphans left to be taken in by relatives and friends. This meant that there would almost certainly be no home available for young Edgar—of necessity he was now a permanent member of the Allan household.

After the signing of the Treaty of Ghent, ending the war between England and America, the Allans took a combination business and pleasure trip to England and Scotland. Edgar had, to all appearances, been taken into John Allan's heart. The merchant's correspondence reflects a kind of parental pride, affection, and hope that he had begun to cherish for this child of "strolling players." But this affection was similar to that shown toward a pet poodle. As long as Edgar acted the role of a charming little boy, smartly tossing his curly head, reciting poems and singing songs while perched upon the highly polished dining-room table, he remained the apple of John Allan's eye.

As soon as the Allans arrived in Scotland, Edgar was enrolled in a very old grammar school, also attended by several of Allan's nephews who lived in the village. The copying of epitaphs from headstones in the graveyard adjacent to the school was an integral part of the instruction in handwriting. This early association gives a macabre hint of Poe's future affinity with death. In many of his poems and short stories, death and the graveyard are major themes. In "The Fall of the House of Usher," for example, the reader is confronted by the corpse-like Lady Madeline returning from her tomb, where she had been prematurely buried. Clawing her way out of the tomb, she comes back to her brother's room and falls upon him, "and in her violent and now final death-agonies, bore him to the floor a corpse . . . ."

The staid grammar school did not suit Edgar's tastes, formed in the warmer, more indulgent social and intellectual atmosphere of Richmond. After the Allans departed for London, where John had business, Edgar lived with one of John's sisters. But his moods, his demands for attention, his tantrums when not allowed his own way, proved too much for his foster aunt. Shortly after the New Year of 1816, she sent him to his foster parents in London. John Allan was exasperated, and even the patient Frances, upon whom Edgar's moods were beginning to wear, was strained beyond endurance. In desperation they enrolled Edgar in Manor House School, at Stoke-Newington, "a misty-looking village of England." Edgar was enrolled under the name of Allan. It was not until he reached young adulthood that he added his original family name of Poe to his adopted name, to become Edgar Allan Poe.

In his story "William Wilson," Poe described the school as an "old and irregular" building surrounded by "a high and solid brick wall, topped with a bed of mortar and broken glass." Dr. Bransby, the headmaster, "with sour visage, and in snuffy habiliments, administered, ferule in hand, the Draconian laws of the academy."

The Reverend John Bransby, the headmaster of the school,

was in later years extremely displeased by Poe's description of him and by the use of his name in "William Wilson." Contrary to the impression Poe gave of the school and of Mr. Bransby in his story, Manor House School boasted an air of happy and wholesome activity, and Mr. Bransby was very much loved and respected by his charges. He had been fond of Edgar but noted that he was spoiled by overindulgent parents. "Allan," he said, "was intelligent, wayward, and wilful." Poe himself said, in the autobiographical "William Wilson": "The ardor, the enthusiasm, and the imperiousness of my disposition, soon rendered me a marked character among my schoolmates . . . ."

The Allans returned to Richmond in 1820, after a five-year stay in England. Edgar had grown into a handsome young man, with a well-developed physique. His brow was prominent and his hair still curly. He was as ready for adventure as any other young person. A friend said of him at this period of his life: "I never saw in him as boy or man a sign of morbidness or melancholy, unless it was when Mrs. Stanard ('Helen') died. . . . Aside from this, cards, raids on orchards and turnip patches, swimming . . . and juvenile masquerades seem to have been the normal order of life."

But though his friends found him a good companion, bubbling over with pranks and mischief, he became at this point in his life increasingly subject to moods of loneliness and depression; morbid thoughts gradually occupied more and more of his consciousness. Edgar himself could not have understood the changes taking place within his mind, his entire being; what had begun to emerge from his mental and physiological turmoil was the artist that would dominate his life from this time on. He knew only that he wanted to be a poet; to express "unthought-like thoughts that are the souls of thought. . . ."

Gradually the boys with whom Edgar attended school became aware of a growing distance between themselves and this once close companion. He withdrew more and more frequently to his room to write verse, or just to daydream. Even John Allan, irritated as he was at Edgar's increasingly strange habits, was forced to admit the excellence of his poetry. He took pride in the boy's work, going so far as to share it with Edgar's teacher at school.

Edgar wrote many of these poems before he reached his mid-teens. They were inspired mainly by the girls who attended a boarding school located across the street from his school. Unknown to the headmistress, he carried on secret correspondence with many of the girls. Edgar also possessed considerable talent as an artist and did pencil sketches of the girls, from whom he asked nothing more than a lock of hair as payment.

A contemporary described Edgar as "trained in all the habits of the most polished society. There was not a brighter, more graceful, or more attractive boy in the city . . . ."

But Edgar's home life was unhappy. There were quarrels with his foster father and a deepening strain between John and Frances caused by Edgar's presence. Allan daily reminded Edgar that it was only his charity that allowed the boy to remain under his roof. Edgar's retorts were equally harsh and intensely bitter.

Edgar's anger turned to rage when he became aware of the fact that Frances, who had been ill for a long time, was going to die. He was now mixing more in society and had heard the gossip about Allan and his affairs with various women in Richmond. Sensitive to the heartbreak that his stepmother had suffered in learning of these affairs, Poe openly criticized Allan for his escapades. Allan in turn grew more demanding of the young man; and in response, Edgar became sullen and uncooperative at home. It was not long before Edgar was packed off to the University of Virginia at Charlottesville. He had been bored with a job as clerk in the firm of Ellis and Allan, and life at the University should have been the perfect solution for all concerned. But it was not to turn out that way.

One of the important people in young Edgar's life was a pretty fifteen-year-old named Elmira Royster. Her large dark eyes and chestnut hair were irresistible to Edgar. The two became secretly engaged before he left for the University, but the romance was doomed. There was parental disapproval on both sides because John Allan had informed Elmira's father that Edgar would not be heir to his fortune. Upon leaving Richmond, Edgar entrusted the family coachman with a letter to Elmira. It was the last message she was to receive from him for a long time.

The University of Virginia had opened its doors a year before Edgar enrolled. It was a radically progressive school for its time, well suited to both his educational needs and his nature. He lived in Room No. 13, West Range, known as "Rowdy Row." He spent most of his time in his room but seldom in deep study. Parties and readings of his own poetry were the order of the day—or night—in No. 13.

Edgar wrote numerous letters home, begging for needed funds. His letters to Elmira, with their declarations of love and complaints about his unanswered letters, never reached their destination. Her mail was intercepted by her father, who eventually forced her to marry a man whom she did not love but who showed more financial promise than Edgar.

Poe was a good student, but the money he needed to remain at the University was not forthcoming. He wrote Allan repeatedly that his cash needs were legitimate and even sent home itemized lists of his expenses. But in return Allan sent just enough money to cover basic needs; nothing extra for unexpected emergencies, a daily occurrence in the life of a university student. Poe was forced to extend his credit in Charlottesville far beyond reasonable bounds just to have enough to eat. In a misdirected effort to obtain extra cash, he gambled; and his consistent losses added to his debts and to his overwrought state of nerves.

Inwardly he was pulled in many directions, frightened and

confused by the unexplained withholding of funds and the silence from Elmira. His emotional turmoil took the form of drinking, to which he turned frantically for temporary release. He was torn between fear of his foster father, whose attitude toward him had grown sadistic, and sympathy for his foster mother. Yet to fellow students he never appeared as anything but composed. Although dissipated, he was always well dressed. He never lacked for companions.

Poe did not like the taste of whiskey, yet the bottle was his only sure escape from his dark forebodings. A friend said he would "seize a full glass, without water or sugar, and send it home at a single gulp." One glass was enough to rouse his nervous nature into a state of wild excitement.

Edgar's greatest desire was to be accepted by his fellow students, whose backgrounds were rooted in the traditions of Virginia's First Families. But his doubts about the acceptability of his own birth drove him to strange behavior. A friend recalled:

On one occasion Poe read a story . . . to some of his friends who, in a spirit of jest, spoke lightly of its merits . . . . His proud spirit would not stand such open rebuke, so in a fit of anger, before his friends could prevent him, he had flung every sheet into a blazing fire, and thus was lost a story of more than ordinary parts which, unlike most of his stories, was intensely amusing, entirely free from his usual somber coloring and sad conclusions merged in a mist of impenetrable gloom.

John Allan came to Charlottesville just before Christmas vacation. After a violent scene with Edgar, he agreed to settle only the debts incurred by Edgar at the University and those for food and clothing. Edgar had to find another way to pay the twenty-five hundred dollars in gambling debts. He declared to a friend that "he was bound by honor to pay . . . every cent of them."

Edgar was now offered the choice of studying law at home, under Allan's watchful eye, or of being turned out on his own. He chose the law. Allan made it clear to Edgar that he would allow him to live at home and study law only if he agreed to follow the rules outlined for him. Edgar rebelled.

After another of their violent quarrels, Edgar fled from the house. It was a cold morning in March, and he had nothing with him except the clothes he was wearing. He remained in hiding for several days at the Courthouse Tavern in Richmond until Frances smuggled money to him through a sympathetic family slave. Allan had turned even the household slaves against Edgar, the ultimate shame for a Southerner.

Under the assumed name of Henri Le Rennet, Poe booked passage to Boston, Massachusetts, on a coastal steamer. He arrived in April, 1827, and promptly found a printer for the publication of his first volume of verse: *Tamerlane and Other Poems.*

The publication of his book took the last of the money sent him by Frances. No published book ever held less promise of success. Distributing it to bookstores and reviewers was difficult. Although he personally placed two copies in the hands of reviewers, there is no known review of the volume—a pamphlet of forty pages bound with paper covers. The title page stated only that its author was "a Bostonian."

Poe was in acute financial need. The United States Army offered an immediate solution to the problem of food and shelter. He enlisted under the name of Edgar A. Perry and gave his age as twenty-two, though he was only eighteen.

On October 31, the battery to which Poe was assigned was ordered to Fort Moultrie, located on Sullivan's Island at the mouth of the Charleston, South Carolina, harbor. He later described this island in his short story "The Gold Bug."

According to Army records, Poe's conduct in the service of his country was excellent. He advanced rapidly to regimental sergeant major. His superior officers, impressed by his outstanding intellectual abilities, recommended that he consider going on to West Point.

Eventually Poe's true identity became known, and John Allan

was informed. Frances was then close to death and Poe was called to her bedside. He arrived too late; Frances, the only stabilizing influence in his life, was gone.

While he was in Richmond, Poe discussed with his foster father the possibility of going to West Point. Allan welcomed the suggestion as a final solution to Edgar's future that would insure his permanent removal from the household. Poe was soon released from the Army, with Allan's permission. His discharge papers stated that he was "sober," an unusual military virtue at that time.

It was several months before Edgar's appointment to West Point became official. During the interim the emotionally unsure young man had no place to stay. He could not return to Richmond and the Allan roof; yet he felt deeply the need of a family and a home. Out of desperation he went to Baltimore, Maryland, to seek out his blood relatives. For some time he had been in correspondence with his brother, William Henry, who lived with their father's sister, Maria Clemm, and her young daughter Virginia. Mrs. Clemm, known affectionately as "Muddie," operated a boardinghouse, its occupants made up mainly of other members of the Poe family.

The addition of Edgar to the household, already bulging with too many Poes, made little difference to Mrs. Clemm. She could always find room in her home and heart for someone in need, particularly if that person was a member of the family. Edgar was taken in with the same warmth that had been offered his brother, now dying of alcoholism and tuberculosis.

In Baltimore the way opened for the young poet to submit his manuscript, *Al Aaraaf, Tamerlane and Minor Poems*, to the *Yankee and Boston Literary Gazette*. The editor commented on Poe's work: "There is a good deal here to justify . . . hope. . . ." Poe said that these were "the very first words of encouragement I ever remember to have heard." John Allan's praise of his early literary efforts was forgotten, the memory wiped out by the subsequent bitterness between them.

In the issue of *Yankee* following the one in which this favorable criticism appeared, there were four pages of selections from his forthcoming book of verse. An accompanying editorial remarked that Poe "will deserve to stand high—very high, in the estimation of the shining brotherhood . . . ."

Al Aaraaf, Tamerlane and Minor Poems, Edgar Allan Poe's second volume of poetry, was published in Baltimore, December, 1829. Although it had many faults, it is considered his first real contribution to American poetry. Most of Poe's poetry is what has been defined as "pure poetry"—poetry that deals with the perceptions of the senses. His poems were created for no other reason than to convey to the reader beauty as he conceived it. An excellent example of this type of poetry is "The Bells," distinctive for its tonal effects of silver, golden, brass, and iron bells. This poem was written toward the end of his life.

On July 1, 1830, Poe took the oath at West Point "to preserve the Constitution of the United States and serve them against all their enemies whomsoever." Poe's roommate described the young cadet: "Poe at that time, though only twenty years of age, had the appearance of being much older. He had a worn, weary discontented look, not easily forgotten by those who were intimate with him. . . . Very early . . . he established a high reputation for genius . . . . The studies of the Academy, Poe utterly ignored. . . . It was evident from the first that he had no intention of going through with the course . . . ."

Disappointment awaited Poe at West Point, as it had at the University of Virginia. His cadet's pay was only twenty-eight dollars a month, to be supplemented by funds and supplies from home. John Allan sent twenty dollars upon Edgar's arrival there, but no further funds, though it was expected that parents of cadets would make a deposit from which the boys could draw for the purchase of books, instruments, uniforms, and other necessities. To be denied the very necessities of life—soap, candles, writing materials, fuel, and proper clothing—was humiliating.

For solace he turned to writing poetry. Among the poems composed during this brief period were "The Sleeper," "To Helen," "Fairy-land," "The Valley of Unrest," and "The City of the Sea." He submitted his new manuscript collection, called *Poems*, to the commanding officer of the Academy.

He received permission to solicit members of the Cadet Corps for subscriptions to the publication of this third book of poetry. Seventy-five cents, to be deducted from the cadet's pay, was charged for each copy. The cadets expected the book to contain a collection of the humorous verse which flowed daily from Poe's room. Poe was aware of their misconception, but knowing that he would not be at the Academy when the book was distributed, he did not allow it to hinder his plan.

Poe deliberately neglected his studies to bring about his dismissal from West Point. He was court-martialed for gross neglect of duty and disobedience to orders. Near the end of March, 1831, he was again established at the Clemm household in the attic room which he shared with his brother William Henry (who would die on August 1, at the age of twenty-four). Upon his return to Baltimore, Poe gave up what little emotional strength he possessed and turned to his aunt for psychological as well as physical support.

The first indication that Poe was turning his pen to a field of writing more lucrative than poetry was the publication of his short story "Metzengerstein" in the Philadelphia *Saturday Courier*. Soon after, his "MS. Found in a Bottle," from his series of short stories, *Tales of the Folio Club*, won the first prize of fifty dollars in a literary contest sponsored by a Baltimore newspaper. For the first time, a relatively large readership was made aware of Poe's work. More important, he gained some influential friends.

The turning point in Poe's career came with an invitation to dine with John P. Kennedy of the Baltimore publishing industry. In reply, Poe sent a note:

Dr Sir,—Your kind invitation to dinner to day has wounded me to the quick. I cannot come—and for reasons of the most humiliating nature [in] my personal appearance. You may conceive my deep mortification in making this disclosure to you—but it was necessary. If you will be my friend so far as to loan me $20 I will call on you to morrow—otherwise it will be impossible, and I must submit to my fate.

To have so freely admitted his dire financial situation was very unlike Poe, whose pride had always prevented him from revealing his personal affairs so openly. This was one of the few times that he was honest with himself and his associates.

Kennedy responded quickly, sending the needed clothing, along with the loan of his personal riding horse. Through Kennedy, Poe made contact with the editor of the *Southern Literary Messenger* in Richmond. After his tale "Berenice" was published in the *Messenger*, the editor invited Poe to join his staff. Poe happily accepted, leaving immediately for Richmond. Although he joined the *Messenger* staff during the summer of 1835, he did not become editor of the publication until December. He was to remain with the *Messenger* for two years. Poe's career as an editor and refiner of the short story had begun. He began to adapt his creative talent to the form most suitable for publication at this period. Through the pages of the periodicals for which he wrote during the years to follow, the reading public was introduced to the detective, or mystery, story, of which Poe was the innovator. In three of Poe's most successful mystery stories: "The Purloined Letter," "The Murders in the Rue Morgue," and "The Mystery of Marie Roget," the central character is C. Auguste Dupin, a French gentleman who has but one weakness—a love of books. He has a unique talent for unraveling the obscure and mysterious, as illustrated in "The Murders in the Rue Morgue," where he discovers that the murderer is an orangutan. In "The Purloined Letter," Dupin, grown even more skilled in his profession, solves the mystery of the theft of an important government document with an ease that delights the reader. In this tale, especially, it becomes obvious why Sir Arthur Conan Doyle confessed that without C. Auguste Dupin there could never have been a Sherlock Holmes.

It might also be added that Poe was expert in creating what is now defined as the psychological fiction "thriller," of which "The Tell-Tale Heart" and "The Pit and the Pendulum" are remarkable examples.

Poe had been unable to find regular employment before he joined the *Messenger* staff. The reasons for this are not clear, though the problem may have been poor health and his use of opium during long periods of emotional and physical collapse. Many literary authorities contend that the evidence of Poe's use of opium during the period between 1831 and 1835 may be found in the work he produced. Later biographers, however, have conjectured that Poe did not use drugs and drank very little alcohol, although it affected him disproportionately. One contemporary account—from Poe's cousin Eliza Herring, who lived with the family for a time—indicates that he did use drugs. Miss Herring said that she had "often seen him decline to take even one glass of wine" but had observed that "for the most part, his periods of excess were occasioned by a free use of opium."

Charles Baudelaire, the French poet, who was deeply influenced by Poe's work and was himself a drug addict, claimed to recognize in several of Poe's tales imagery saturated with descriptions of dreams and delusions typical of the opium user. A specific example is found in "Ligeia," where Poe describes "the radiance of an opium-dream—an airy and spirit-lifting vision more wildly divine than the phantasies which hovered about the slumbering souls of the daughters of Delos."

Upon his return to Richmond, Poe realized that the past must be forgotten. John Allan was dead. The memory of their quarrels and the bitterness of loss and disappointment must be allowed to die too. Life in Richmond was a marked relief from the drab years in Baltimore. Poe was as welcome as ever in the homes of childhood friends, whose sympathies about past events in the Allan household lay with Edgar. He was included in Richmond's endless social whirl, a happy relief from a long day's work. The most pleasing feature of Richmond society was the lively interest in cultural matters, especially literature. He gave numerous readings of his own poetry, along with selections from popular authors.

The *Messenger*'s editor quickly discerned Poe's capacity as an editor and left him in charge of the office while he traveled over the state soliciting subscriptions. Through the combined efforts of Poe's brilliant pen and the editor's persistence in recruiting subscribers, the *Messenger*'s subscription list increased rapidly. But Poe's drinking caused him to be dismissed, although the editor took him back, writing in response to Poe's appeal for a second chance: "That you are sincere in all your promises, I firmly believe. . . . If you should . . . again be an assistant in my office, it must be expressly understood by us that all engagements on my part would be dissolved, the moment you get drunk. No man is safe who drinks before breakfast!"

In May, 1836, Poe was married to Virginia Clemm, and the couple, with Virginia's mother, "Muddie," took up residence in Richmond. There is some evidence that a secret marriage had taken place between Edgar and Virginia a year earlier. Virginia was only fourteen at the time of their marriage and in many ways a strange bride for Poe. He had had several other romantic interests, all suitable to his age. Yet Virginia's almost infantile mind and body held a strange fascination for him, which he could not explain to himself. Many of the author's fictional heroines were clearly modeled after the perennially ailing Virginia. The "lost Ulalume," Eleonora who saw "the finger of Death . . . upon her bosom," Lady Madeline who had "succumbed . . . to the prostrating power of the destroyer," the "beautiful Annabel

Lee," and Berenice, "gorgeous yet fantastic beauty!" all bear a strong resemblance to the pale Virginia. The marriage provided Poe with the emotional security of an established home, complete with wife, mother-in-law, and a cat purring at the fireside.

Poe rapidly became known in magazine circles as an editor and writer who stood for progress, originality, and genius. His ability as a literary critic was considered exceptional. He could winnow from the avalanche of books, even then pouring from the presses of American and European publishers, what would stand the test of time to become solid literature from what has proven to be trash. He was able to separate himself from the mawkish sentimentalism prevalent in much of the American and English literature of the period. He was the first American critic, for example, to see the enduring qualities of Hawthorne's *Twice Told Tales*. His work on the *Messenger* broadened the scope and influence of the magazine and brought it into national prominence as a literary publication.

In the process of developing the *Messenger*'s format, Poe evolved firm ideas of what a nationally oriented magazine, of which there were none in the United States at that time, should include. Unlike many magazine editors and writers of his day, he did not write down to his readers, whom he addressed as if they were all interested in serious literature and genuine criticism. Although he was not entirely correct about what his readers—the first generation to come to maturity under the public school system—wanted in a magazine, Poe was ahead of his time in his concept of what a magazine with readers drawn from every educational level and representative of every kind of literary taste should offer. He knew instinctively that a publication of this magnitude would have to be organized and operated from New York or Philadelphia.

Poe resigned from the *Southern Literary Messenger* in January, 1837—an unwise move. He was well established in an editorial position and doing reasonably well financially. His reputation as an editor and writer was spreading to many quarters, including New England, then the literary center of the United States. The financial depression of 1837 had taken its toll in the New York publishing industry. When Poe arrived in New York in February of that year, with Virginia and Muddie at his side, the depression was at its height. Many newspapers and magazines had closed their doors. Only the old reliable authors were a sure bet: Cooper, Bryant, Irving. But Poe—no, the risk was too great.

In spite of his good contacts in publishing circles, Poe found no steady employment. He did some occasional hack work; with nothing else available it put some food on the table. Not all of the blame for his difficulty in finding work could be placed on the financial depression. Poe made it clear to potential employers that he would accept nothing less than an editorial position. He might have accepted whatever employment was available, or temporary work, if only to get a start. He could, for instance, have taken a job as clerk, for which he had been trained during summer months when he worked for his foster father in Richmond. But he made no such moves. Muddie did nothing to encourage him in such practical endeavors as this, preferring to wring her hands over "poor Eddie" and weaken him further by willingly begging food wherever she could.

Now with time on his hands, Poe set about completing his only novel, *The Narrative of Arthur Gordon Pym, of Nantucket*, published in July, 1838. It was an account of "a Mutiny and Atrocious Butchery on board the American Brig Grampus, on her Way to the South Seas." This was Poe's fourth published book and his first volume of prose. Although he had never been to the South Seas, his description of that part of the world, as well as other geographical points mentioned in the narrative, were true enough to lead one reader to remark, "I lent it to a friend . . . a brother of Dr. O. W. Holmes, yet he is so completely deceived by the minute accuracy of some of the details . . . that though an intelligent and shrewd man he will not be persuaded that it is a fictitious work." Poe's research had been thorough.

Poe found no promise for expansion of his career in New York City and was forced to make another move. The family was close to starvation. By the late summer of 1838, Poe was near desperation. He borrowed money and went to Philadelphia in search of work. It was not until May, 1839, that he found a permanent position. He became editor of *Burton's Gentleman's Magazine*. In the meantime, he worked on several short stories. These were included in his second book of prose, *Tales of the Grotesque and Arabesque*, which appeared in 1840. It was published in two volumes and comprised some of Poe's most imaginative Gothic tales, among them "Metzengerstein," "MS. Found in a Bottle," "Morella," "Ligeia," "William Wilson," "The Fall of the House of Usher," and "Berenice."

After leaving *Burton's* and becoming editor of *Graham's Magazine*, Poe and his family experienced their most prosperous period; but it was short-lived. Poe saw that the publisher of *Graham's* was not going to fulfill two fundamental points in their contract: He was not going to give promised financial backing to the establishment of the national magazine of which Poe had long dreamed, nor was he going to take him in as a partner of *Graham's*.

When the pressure of fear and frustration began to bear in upon him, Poe reverted to his old drinking habits. Morbid self-pity cast a shadow over his whole being, and he was beyond reason or being reasoned with. To add to his problems, Virginia became seriously ill with tuberculosis. She appeared to improve, and then suffered repeated relapses, always into a more serious condition.

After long hours of watching by her bedside, Poe seemed completely deranged. He escaped from the house into the night, rambling aimlessly. Emotionally he could not stand this clash with reality; the problem of Virginia's illness coupled with disappointments about his career was overwhelming. Alcohol offered the only relief from this labyrinth of madness. It took very little alcohol to make Poe forget his problems and give him a temporary sense of well-being. He wrote a friend: "I drank, God only knows how often or how much. . . . As a matter of course, my enemies referred the insanity to the drink rather than the drink to the insanity."

A fellow editor described one of Poe's alcoholic deliriums:

> He walked the streets, in madness or melancholy, with lips moving in indistinct curses, or with eyes upturned in passionate prayers . . . for their happiness who were at the moment the objects of his idolatry; or with his glance introverted to a heart gnawed with anguish, and with a face shrouded in gloom, he would brave the wildest storms; and at night, with drenched garments and arms wildly beating the wind and rain he would speak as if to spirits that at such times only could be evoked by him . . . .

Poe would disappear for days on an alcoholic binge, only to be sought out by the anxious Muddie, who brought him home and nursed him back to a relative degree of sanity. "His dissipation was too notorious to be denied," a friend said of him. As a result of his drinking, the publisher for whom he worked retracted his agreement with him. He appreciated Poe's genius and was sympathetic to his problems; but still, he had a magazine to operate. He was forced to let him go but continued to pay for his work, contributed regularly to the magazine.

Poe's dismissal from *Graham's* in May, 1842, left the family in immediate poverty. He had never been wise in handling his salary, and, aware of this weakness, had faithfully turned his paychecks over to Muddie to budget. But even her practical wisdom was not enough to save the amount needed to tide them over the long periods during which Poe was in a condition of helpless intoxication. The comfortable, well-furnished home which Poe, Virginia, and Muddie had established had to be given up for more humble quarters.

Hack work, the occasional sale of a story, and Muddie's ability to prevail upon the sympathy of friends and strangers kept the family alive. Muddie also pawned their furniture, piece by piece, until the house was barren except for some painted chairs the landlady held in lieu of rent owed.

At this time Virginia had another relapse. There was no food left in the house. A collection was taken up in the office of *Graham's Magazine* and fifteen dollars was entrusted to Muddie in an effort to help the family.

Poe was at the end of his rope in Philadelphia. He was now known throughout the journalistic profession in that city as unreliable and difficult to deal with. He could not return to Richmond or Baltimore because his reputation was known in those places also. His attacks on Longfellow and the New England writers marked Boston off the list. New York City was the only literary center where he might make a new start.

When Poe and Virginia boarded the train for New York, he had only eleven dollars in his pocket. Muddie was left in Philadelphia to dispose of their few remaining possessions. She followed later with Catarina, the family cat.

Soon after arriving in New York, Poe sold "The Balloon Hoax" to the *New York Sun*. It made its appearance in an astonishing manner. The *Sun*'s morning issue of April 13, 1844, carried an item that appeared to have been received just as the paper went to press: an announcement that a balloon, which had drifted on air currents across the Atlantic, had been sighted off the coast. An Extra edition was promised within a few hours to give full details of the event.

The Extra carried Poe's story, printed as a news scoop. No one in the crowd that looked up anxiously at the sky during the hurried reading of the Extra guessed that the incident was a well-planned hoax. Many people even reported that they saw the balloon. Others just stared skyward in disbelief.

"The Balloon Hoax" is one of Poe's better-known works of science fiction. Poe made an important contribution to science fiction, as he did with other writing forms—Gothic, detective, psychological thriller.

After this dazzling display, Poe was once again dependent upon hack work for a living. Editorial positions were hard to find in New York. Summer came with its oppressive heat; Virginia had to be moved to the country and cooler air. Settled in an old house on Bloomingdale Road, six miles from the city, Poe set about the task of completing "The Raven," a long, somber, brooding poem on which he had been working since before he left Philadelphia.

The mood of the poem reflected the mood of its author: a darkening view of the future, a feeling of dejection and futility which Poe found more and more difficult to throw off. This is clearly evident in the poem's last stanza:

And the Raven, never flitting, still is sitting, *still* is sitting
On the pallid bust of Pallas just above my chamber door;
And his eyes have all the seeming of a demon's that is dreaming,
And the lamp-light o'er him streaming throws his shadow on
    the floor;
And my soul from out that shadow that lies floating on the floor
          Shall be lifted—nevermore!

Sick and discouraged, Poe recoiled from the prospect of returning to the daily routine of a regular job. Fall approached and he made no attempt to go to the city to find work. Muddie, who was understanding but a weakening influence where "Eddie" was concerned, took matters into her own hands and went to New York to find employment for him. At Poe's suggestion she called on N. P. Willis, the editor of the New York *Mirror*. Willis later wrote that "she excused her errand by mentioning that he was ill, and that her daughter was a confirmed invalid."

Muddie made her appeal so pathetic that the editor did not have the heart to turn down her request. He knew of Poe's reputation; his debauchery, his temperamental habits had all preceded him to New York from Philadelphia. But the editor was also familiar with Poe's genius, his ability as an editor, critic, and writer. He agreed to hire Poe. Poe, out of gratitude, turned over a new leaf. He worked hard and kept regular hours at the *Mirror*'s office. He poured his genius into the development and improvement of the publication and made a special effort to encourage and assist young, unknown writers. He even responded agreeably to the publisher's suggestions that he make his critical remarks less harsh and turn his bitter irony into a more cheerful tone.

When the *Broadway Journal*, a weekly publication, began operations the following year, Poe joined the staff as an editorial assistant and later became a partner. His departure from the *Mirror*'s staff was marked by the fact that he left voluntarily, much to the editor's disappointment. He had proved an exceptionally good employee during the year he had worked there, and the editor was sorry to lose so valuable and dependable a man. Poe had evidently stopped his excessive drinking during this period.

"The Raven" was published a short time after Poe left the *Mirror*. The poem was an overnight success and is one of his works which assures him lasting fame. Its immediate and widespread success can be compared with only one other American poem: "Old Ironsides" by Oliver Wendell Holmes. Before Poe left the *Mirror*, he arranged with Willis for an advance and anonymous publication of "The Raven," in the *Mirror*. This was the first appearance of the poem in print. It later appeared in *The American Whig Review* and several other publications.

Poe suddenly found himself a celebrity; he and his autograph were sought after, and his manuscripts became collectors' items. Yet his fame did not change Poe's financial status at all. He was paid ten dollars for the poem. Ironically, the manuscript sold in London in 1929 for one hundred thousand dollars.

In the early part of March, 1845, Poe became co-editor of the *Broadway Journal*. Several months later he bought, with borrowed money, a one-third interest in the publication. His goal of owning his own publication was very close to attainment when he became highhanded and forcibly took control of the office. One of his partners withdrew in disgust, and Poe bought out the other with money he again borrowed, adding to his indebtedness. He was now the owner and publisher of his own weekly publication; his dream was a reality.

Poe had a psychological quirk which is difficult to understand. On two other occasions during his career he had been on the verge of ownership of a publication. Each time, at almost the moment of success and for no understandable reason, he turned to excessive drinking and ruined his opportunity. Now that he actually held the reins of ownership in his hands, he again began drinking. He defaulted on his notes. The *Journal* rapidly deteriorated under Poe's ownership. Although he had proved himself a fine editor of other publications, he did not have the skill to manage the financial affairs of a publication. His drinking was also a contributing factor. Poe was sole owner and operator of the *Journal* from October 24, 1845, to January 3, 1846, when the last issue appeared.

Conditions of poverty had become so extreme in the home that Poe and Muddie were embarrassed to receive visitors. In May, 1846, they moved to a cottage in Fordham, not far from the city. They had only a few pieces of furniture, and a bed had to be left at their former address in payment of overdue rent. Yet the Fordham cottage, according to friends, "had an air of gentility that must have been lent to it by the presence of its inmates."

The family settled in for the winter. Virginia lay dying in a small unheated room on the first floor. While summer and early fall remained, Muddie had kept food on the table, if only a salad of dandelion greens or a bowl of turnip soup. In the city, summer or winter, there were always friends to whom she could appeal when all other resources failed; in Fordham, a farming community where houses were scattered miles apart, the Poes lived in total isolation now that the snow had begun to fall.

A woman friend in New York City felt compelled to come through the snow to see the Poes in early December. It took persistence to get her horse-drawn sled through the drifts. At the cottage she found conditions that would have softened the most calloused hearts. The house, though as clean and neat as Muddie could make it, was unheated. There was a wood-burning stove in the kitchen and a fireplace in the living room, but no fuel. Poe was too stupefied by his own deteriorating health to search for fuel in the surrounding woods. Virginia's illness had become his obsession, and even Muddie, ordinarily possessed of a keen presence of mind, had but one objective: to keep life in Virginia's body. The visitor later recorded:

> I saw her in her bed-chamber.
> There was no clothing on the bed, which was only straw, but a snow-white counterpane and sheets. . . . She lay in the straw bed, wrapped in her husband's great coat, with a large tortoiseshell cat in her bosom. The wonderful cat seemed conscious of her great usefulness. The coat and the cat were the sufferer's only means of warmth, except as her husband held her hands, and her mother her feet.

Upon returning to the city, the friend gained assistance for the Poes from anyone willing to listen. Food, bed clothing, a featherbed, and fuel, along with sixty dollars in cash, were sent to the family immediately. There followed a constant flow of gifts of money and food from friends in the city until Virginia's death, a month later, on January 30, 1847.

After Virginia died, Poe "never liked to be alone," according to Mrs. Clemm. He was subject to spells of delirium and hours of wandering, from which he returned with no memory of where he had been or what he had done. Poe lived as a recluse during the year that followed. He had ceased to write, and he spent the nights prowling around the graveyard where Virginia was buried. But in 1848 his letters began to reflect a great need for feminine sympathy and companionship. The first woman with whom he fell in love after Virginia's death was Sarah Helen Whitman of Rhode Island, the "Seeress of Providence."

Mrs. Whitman was a beautiful woman but a neurotic like her suitor. A widow, she is said to have suffered from a chronic heart ailment. She was a spiritualist who spent most of her time "communicating" with the spirit world. Mrs. Whitman played her role of spiritual seer to the limit and assumed a specter-like habit of gliding about, almost as if she had wheels in place of feet. She draped herself in scarves which floated behind her as she moved across the room, always dimly lit, and there was ever the faint odor of ether about her person, as if to suggest an antidote for the too harsh realities of daily existence. In all respects she was the ideal Poe heroine, and for a brief time appeared the perfect replacement for the pallid Virginia, the "lost Ulalume."

Poe's courtship of Mrs. Whitman was whirlwind, their first rendezvous taking place in a cemetery. She eventually refused him, after which he attempted suicide. He rambled from New York to Philadelphia, to Baltimore, and to Richmond, writing and lecturing.

Upon reaching Richmond he saw again his old sweetheart, Sarah Elmira Royster, to whom he had been secretly engaged before he left to attend the University of Virginia. Elmira, now Mrs. Alexander Shelton, had been recently widowed. The romance was renewed, and Poe planned to remain in Richmond. Muddie was to join him and make her home with him and Elmira. Poe's health was seriously impaired from his heavy drinking. A Richmond doctor warned him that he must give up drinking, which he agreed to do.

A short time before he and Elmira were to be married, Poe planned a brief lecture tour to New York City. On the way he was to stop in Philadelphia to deliver a manuscript he had edited. Elmira wrote that the day before he was to leave "he was very sad, and complained of being quite sick." "I felt his pulse," she continued, "and found he had considerable fever, and did not think it probable he would be able to start the next morning."

Elmira underestimated Poe's recuperative energies. Later in the evening he dined with friends, who accompanied him to the boat. They reported him to be sober and in excellent spirits when they parted from him. But two unusual things happened as he left Richmond: he forgot to take his luggage with him, and though now under the constant care of a doctor, he did not tell his doctor he was going on a trip which would last at least two weeks.

Little is known of Poe's activities after he arrived in Baltimore, from which he was to proceed to Philadelphia. On the first day he called on a friend who was not at home. The servant who opened the door noted that Poe was slightly intoxicated at the time.

After a lapse of several days, on the afternoon of October 3, 1849, he was found, by a printer, who recognized him, in an alcoholic stupor in a tavern. Poe was conscious enough to ask for a friend, who was summoned by messenger. In the note dispatched, the printer explained:

"There is a gentleman, rather the worse for wear, at Ryan's 4th ward polls, who goes under the cognomen of Edgar A. Poe, and who appears in great distress, and he says he is acquainted with you, and I assure you he is in need of immediate assistance."

The friend, who happened to be a medical doctor, hurried to the barroom and found Poe in a shocking state:

His face was haggard . . . bloated, and unwashed, his hair unkempt and his whole physique repulsive. His expansive forehead . . . and those full-orbed and mellow, yet soulful eyes for which he was so noticeable when himself, now lusterless . . . shaded from view by a rusty, almost brimless, tattered and ribbonless palm leaf hat. His clothing consisted of a sack-coat of thin and sleezy black alpaca, ripped more or less at intervals of its seams, and faded and soiled, and pants . . . half worn and badly fitting, if they could be said to fit at all. He wore neither vest nor neck cloth, while the bosom of his shirt was both crumpled and badly soiled.

How pathetic this description of Poe's appearance is when contrasted with one written by a Baltimore editor fifteen years before. Upon meeting the then young poet, the editor commented:

His figure was remarkably good, and he carried himself erect and well, as one who had been trained to it. He was dressed in black, and his frock coat was buttoned to the throat, where it met the black stock, then almost universally worn. Not a particle of white was visible. Coat, hat, boots, and gloves had evidently seen their best days, but so far as mending and brushing go, everything had been done . . . to make them presentable. On most men his clothes would have looked shabby and seedy, but there was something about this man that prevented one from criticizing his garments . . . . Gentleman was written all over him.

Poe was immediately taken to Washington Hospital by his doctor friend. He had slipped into unconsciousness and remained so until the next day, when he rallied slightly. He lingered on in a state of alcoholic delirium, and died on Sunday, October 7, 1849, at the age of forty. Elmira Shelton's influence prevented the cause of death from being recorded as delirium tremens. A cousin who attended his funeral remarked: "Edgar had seen so much of sorrow, had so little reason to be satisfied with life that, to him, the change can scarcely be said to be a misfortune."

Poe was a man to whom the world of dreams (often the world of nightmares) was more real than the actual world around him. He dreamed "dreams no mortal ever dared to dream before"—to quote from "The Raven." These lines from his poem "A Dream within a Dream" would have made a fitting epitaph for him:

> You are not wrong, who deem
> That my days have been a dream . . . .
> *All* that we see or seem
> Is but a dream within a dream.

Suggested Reading*

POE ANTHOLOGIES:

Complete Stories and Poems of Edgar Allan Poe. New York: Doubleday & Co.†

Edgar Allan Poe Stories. Great Writers Collection. New York: Platt & Munk, 1961.

Eight Tales of Terror. Edited by John P. Roberts. New York: Scholastic Book Services.†

Introduction to Poe: A Thematic Reader. Edited by Eric W. Carlson. Glenview, Ill.: Scott, Foresman & Co., 1967.

Narrative of Arthur Gordon Pym, The. Illus. Boston: David R. Godine, 1973.

Pit and the Pendulum and Five Other Tales, The. Illus. by Rick Schreiter. New York: Franklyn Watts, 1967.

Poems of Edgar Allan Poe. Edited by Dwight Macdonald. New York: Thomas Y. Crowell Co., 1965.

Purloined Letter, The—The Murders in the Rue Morgue. Illus. by Rick Schreiter. New York: Franklin Watts, 1966.

Selections from Poe's Marginalia. Folcroft, Pa.: Folcroft Library Editions, 1973.

Tales and Poems of Edgar Allan Poe. Illus. by Russell Hoban. Afterword by Clifton Fadiman. New York: The Macmillan Co., 1963.

BOOKS ABOUT EDGAR ALLAN POE:

Benet, Laura. *Young Edgar Allan Poe.* New York: Dodd, Mead & Co., 1961.

Bittner, William. *Poe: A Biography.* Boston: Little, Brown & Co., 1962.

Hoff, Rhoda. *Four American Poets.* New York: Henry Z. Walck, 1969.

Hoffman, Daniel. *Poe Poe Poe Poe Poe Poe Poe.* New York: Doubleday & Co., 1972.

Porgess, Irwin. *Edgar Allan Poe.* Philadelphia: Chilton Book Co., 1963.

Winwar, Frances. *The Haunted Palace: A Life of Edgar Allan Poe.* New York: Harper & Row, 1959.

* The author has listed popular editions for convenient reference.
† Publication date not available.

Herman Melville

Herman Melville
/"Call Me Ishmael"

... when I go to sea, I go as a simple sailor, right before the mast, plumb down into the forecastle, aloft there to the royal mast-head. True, they rather order me about some, and make me jump from spar to spar, like a grasshopper in a May meadow. And at first, this sort of thing is unpleasant enough. It touches one's sense of honor, particularly if you come of an old established family in the land, the Van Rensselaers, or Randolphs, or Hardicanutes. And more than all, if just previous to putting your hand into the tar-pot, you have been lording it as a country schoolmaster, making the tallest boys stand in awe of you. The transition is a keen one, I assure you, from a schoolmaster to a sailor . . . .

The words of Ishmael, narrator of *Moby Dick*, could have described author Herman Melville's feelings as a young sailor and his relation to the sea. Like Ishmael, Melville came "of an old established family in the land" and had "been lording it as a country schoolmaster" before he set forth on his first voyage aboard the "St. Lawrence" on June 5, 1839.

Although Melville spent only five years as a sailor, these years laid the foundation for his career as a writer. At an age when most young men destined to become authors would have devoted themselves to study, writing, and association with other young intellectuals, Melville was serving as an able-bodied seaman, companioning with the illiterate and exploited seamen of nineteenth-century merchant vessels, whalers, and men-of-war. As Melville himself said, he had substituted a whaling ship for Yale and Harvard. But his success and appeal as a writer grew out of this unique education.

Herman Melville was born August 1, 1819, in New York City. His father, Allan Melville, operated an import business in the city. The elder Melville spoke French fluently and traveled throughout Europe to buy the silks, taffetas, ribbons, gloves, and leghorn hats sold in his store. His New York City was that of new writers, new books, new plays, "native" operas, new schools of historical and landscape painting. John Jacob Astor, fur trader and financier, was laying the foundations for the future capital of American finance, and author James Fenimore Cooper was writing *The Spy* and his other early novels. Washington Irving, a native of New York though living abroad, was producing works like "Rip Van Winkle" and *The Conquest of Granada*; and William Cullen Bryant, poet and editor of the *New York Post*, was lecturing at the new Athenaeum, expounding upon poetry and defending the "still unaccepted romantic writers."

This was an era of marked opulence, artistically and financially, and the senior Melville, like many businessmen of the period, overinvested his money. In the summer of 1830, a business in which he was a silent partner failed. Within days, Allan Melville, proprietor of the elegant import and merchandising establishment on Pine Street, was bankrupt. Every effort to save his business failed, and lawsuits were filed against him. In embarrassed confusion and haste, he moved his family to Albany, New York, where they lived with relatives. With money borrowed from his father, Allan started a factory to manufacture fur caps.

It was at this juncture in the fortunes of the Melville family that Herman's parents' emotional and religious backgrounds came to the fore. Allan, who had been extremely liberal in his concept of religion, now fanatically embraced the Calvinistic doctrine of the Presbyterian Church in which he had been raised. His wife's frivolous, indulgent nature gave way to a deep brooding on man's fate as a sinner doomed to eternal damnation and punishment. Maria Melville had been reared in the Dutch Reformed Church, which is based on the doctrine of Calvinism.

Before the Melville finances were depleted, religious observances had occupied a normally important place in the household routine, along with the endless social whirl in which the family reveled. But now attention to religious matters increased. Daily, there were formal family gatherings for prayer and meditation, along with the reading aloud of religious tracts and a somber keeping of church duties on Sunday.

Herman's father died in 1832, his mind deranged by worry and overwork. He left his wife and children almost penniless, except for the small income from the factory. After her husband's death, Maria became harsh and possessive. She was overly demanding of her children. At a time of life when his father's once liberal grasp of religion would have been an important influence on his intellectual development, Herman fell completely under the restrictive doctrine of Calvinism as now practiced by his mother. This created within him a dark, foreboding concept of life and influenced the books he later wrote.

Sixteen-year-old Gansevoort, Herman's older brother, was placed in charge of the factory. Herman left school to assist him. Together they operated the factory for five years. During a brief period of prosperity in the business, Herman was enrolled at the Albany Classical School. During less prosperous periods, both boys managed to further their education through the Albany Young Men's Association for Mutual Improvement.

Fortunately for Herman, the Association maintained a large library. When he was not at the factory, he was there, reading and making good use of other educational facilities offered by the Association. Although Herman disliked school, he developed into a promising student. His grades at the Albany Classical School had not been high, but a professor remembered him as a fine writer of themes.

When the financial depression of 1837 struck, Gansevoort was forced to close the factory. Since Albany offered no further opportunities for a career, he went to New York City to study law. Herman secured a post as schoolmaster in a one-room schoolhouse near Pittsfield, Massachusetts.

Although there were only thirty students in the school, they were unruly and difficult to teach. They could not work even simple problems in arithmetic. By the end of the school year, Herman was extremely discouraged. He gave up teaching and returned to his home in Albany.

He was promised an engineering job on the Erie Canal project, but this would demand further education. The family's poor financial condition left little extra money to help him through school. He was anxious to prepare for a career not only to satisfy his own longings but also, eventually, to contribute to his mother's and sisters' support. The women had already cast off false pride enough to take in sewing. But further measures were needed if the family was to have enough to eat and a roof over their heads.

Rents were lower in Lansingburg, N.Y., than in Albany, and the Academy there offered the courses in engineering and surveying that Herman sought. The Melvilles moved to the town, which overlooked the Hudson River, and Herman enrolled at the Academy. After a year of study, he graduated. But the promised career with the Erie Canal project failed to materialize. He could not return to teaching until the following fall, so to support himself for the next few months he signed on the passenger ship "St. Lawrence," bound for Liverpool, England.

This fateful day for Herman was suggestive of his later novel, *Redburn*. Like his character Redburn, Herman found it "was with a heavy heart and full eyes, that my poor mother parted with me; perhaps she thought me an erring and a willful boy, and perhaps I was; but if I was, it had been a hard-hearted world, and hard times that had made me so."

Herman's escape to the sea not only betokened his future as a writer of sea stories but also removed him from what was becoming an overpowering family situation. After Gansevoort went to New York City to study law, Herman was the oldest son remaining at home. This placed upon him a severe burden: that of being the main provider for his mother, four sisters, and two younger brothers. His mother also looked upon him as the emotional stay of the family, a demand too great for the seventeen-year-old Herman. As he wrote in his largely autobiographical *Redburn*, "So I broke loose from their arms, and not daring to look behind, ran away as fast as I could . . . ."

As the character Redburn, Herman recalled:

It was early on a raw, cold, damp morning toward the end of spring, and the world was before me; stretching away a long muddy road, lined with comfortable houses, whose inmates were taking their sunrise naps, heedless of the wayfarer passing. The cold drops of drizzle trickled down my leather cap, and mingled with a few hot tears on my cheeks.

A new world opened before him as the ship put out to sea: a world in which the captain of the ship was master of every soul on board.

As soon as New York Harbor was out of sight, the crew were ordered to assemble on deck. They were told their first duty would be to the commands of the captain. The change of occupation was a shock to Herman. He knew that a sailor's pay was pitifully small and that as a crew member he would possess almost no human rights, but the transition was difficult. His former life, by comparison, had been soft, his manner of living genteel.

Among other things, Herman had to learn the language of the sea. He found it harsh and meaningless at first. Before the ship left port, he was ordered, as he records in *Redburn*, to "slush down the main-top mast." The mate explained, and not too gently, to the baffled landlubber, "Look you, youngster. Look up to that long pole there—d'ye see it? that piece of a tree there, you timber-head—well—take this bucket here, and go up the rigging —that rope-ladder there—do you understand?—and dab this slush all over the mast, and look out for your head if one drop falls on deck."

But at sea, there was not time to explain every order and illustrate how it was to be carried out. Herman learned by observing the more experienced crewmen work. The first and most humiliating order Herman received from the Chief Mate, after the ship reached open seas, was to "clean out that pig-pen in the long-boat . . . ."

The author reflected in *Redburn*: "Was this then the beginning of my sea-career? set to cleaning out a pig-pen, the very first thing?" (Livestock was carried aboard ships for food, until modern refrigeration made this unnecessary.)

Morning began at 4:00 A.M. aboard the "St. Lawrence." Before breakfast, which consisted of corn mush, salt beef, hard biscuit, and black coffee, "an order was given to wash down the decks." Herman thought "this . . . the most foolish thing in the world, and besides that it was the most uncomfortable." No one had instructed him, before leaving port, to take boots for this operation, and his bare feet were numb with cold.

Ship's gossip was exchanged around the scuttlebutt, a wooden barrel from which the men drew their daily ration of drinking water. Off-duty crew members gathered at the scuttlebutt to spin yarns and impress one another with past exploits.

"As for me," Melville wrote in *Redburn*, "I was but a boy; and at any time aboard ship, a boy is expected to keep quiet, do what he is bid, never presume to interfere, and seldom to talk, unless spoken to. For merchant sailors have a great idea of their dignity, and superiority to *greenhorns* and *landsmen* . . . . I kept thus quiet, and had very little to say . . . ."

Most of the work to keep the "St. Lawrence" in repair was

done at sea. In port, the crew were busy with the unloading and loading of cargo. In making repairs, Melville, along with the rest of the crew, became adept at renewing old materials. Old rope, worn beyond use, was taken apart and the pieces spliced together to make rope yarn. This was spun into marline and used to mend other rope. Rust had to be chipped from the anchor and chain, and the sides of the ship painted where salt air and water had eaten away the original paint. Herman viewed this work as "most monotonous, and to me a most uncongenial and irksome business."

He soon realized a strong back was needed to make a sailor worth sixteen dollars a month. The ability to carry out many orders quickly and efficiently was also a necessity. But Herman "endeavored to bear it all like a young philosopher, and whiled away the tedious hours by gazing through a port-hole while my hands were plying, and repeating Lord Byron's Address to the Ocean . . . ."

"As I began to learn my sailor duties," he wrote in *Redburn*, "and show activity in running aloft, the men, I observed, treated me with a little more consideration, though not at all relaxing in a certain air of professional superiority." A sailor had to be carpenter, sailmaker, blacksmith, and a nimble-footed athlete all rolled into one, and work no less than fourteen hours a day.

Herman's free hours were spent in the forecastle, a cabin in the forward section of the ship. This was the crew's living quarters. It was crowded with bunks, sea chests, and off-duty men trying to sleep. But the pounding of waves on the ship's hull and tramping feet on the deck above made it noisy.

How great a change it was for Herman, from the spacious and commodious home of his childhood to the crude, cramped, and usually foul-smelling forecastle. Even when his family's resources were at their lowest ebb, he had never experienced living conditions so depressing. The men with whom he shared these quarters had been sailors for many years; their speech was harsh and their manners rude. Yet they came to forgive Herman his good English and more refined habits; by the time the ship reached Liverpool, they considered him *almost* as capable a sailor as themselves.

When Melville returned to Lansingburg, he found conditions in his mother's household little different; if anything, they were worse. His mother's morose attitude toward life had so deepened that Herman wished he had remained a sailor.

He took a teaching post at Greenbush, a village thirteen miles from Lansingburg. Throughout the winter of 1840, he walked home every weekend to do what he could for his family and to bring a small offering to the budget. In June, 1840, he went west to Galena, Illinois, hoping to find a more promising career. He returned a few months later, disappointed. He then joined Gansevoort in New York City and searched for a job.

The most popular book that year was *Two Years Before the Mast*, by Richard Henry Dana. Melville read it and became so enraptured with this South Sea adventure that he longed for similar action. It was not long before he signed on the whaling ship "Acushnet," bound for the South Pacific. She sailed from Buzzard's Bay, Massachusetts, January 3, 1841. Five years would elapse before Melville again sighted the shores of the United States.

On the first page of his book *Typee*, Melville outlined a somewhat exaggerated picture of a sailor's life aboard a passenger ship such as the "St. Lawrence." By contrast to what he was to experience on board the "Acushnet," life on the "St. Lawrence" must have seemed, even at its poorest, paradise in retrospect: "Oh! ye state-room sailors, who make so much ado about a fourteen-days' passage across the Atlantic . . . what would ye say to our six months out of sight of land?"

Although a sailor's lot, even aboard the "St. Lawrence," was not simple, Melville's rights as a human being on the "Acushnet" did not exist. Melville describes this condition in *Typee*:

"The usage on board of her was tyrannical . . . and her cruises were unreasonably protracted. The captain was the author of these abuses; it was vain to think that he would either remedy them, or alter his conduct, which was arbitrary and violent in the extreme."

If the "Acushnet" returned from the voyage fully loaded with whale oil, the cargo would be worth thirty thousand dollars. The ship's articles insured each sailor a share of these profits. Melville's share might be as much as two hundred dollars, if he did not draw too heavily on the the slop chest for clothing and tobacco during the voyage. The slop chest was the ship's store, and any items drawn from it by a sailor were paid for out of his wages.

Action aboard the "Acushnet" was much like that which took place aboard the whaling ship "Pequod" described by Melville in his novel *Moby Dick*. As the "Acushnet" neared the Equator, a lookout was stationed atop the highest mast of the ship. While he watched for whale spouts, every man on board was alert for his cry, "There she blows! there! there! there! she blows! she blows!"

"Where-away?" shouted the excited sailors at the long-awaited signal.

"On the lee-beam, about two miles off! a school of them!"

The crewmen had already begun their scramble for the small boats "dropped into the sea; while, with a dexterous, off-handed daring, unknown in any other vocation, the sailors, goat-like, leaped down the rolling ship's side into the tossed boats below."

The whale might be half as long as the ship, and a third as wide, but this did not deter the dauntless seamen. Each of the small boats was rowed by four men, and from one a harpooner would drive his harpoon into the whale. It took courage to row the tiny boat close to the great mammal and wait while the harpooner struck the deadly blow.

The harpoon was fastened to a long rope secured, at the other end, to the boat. After the harpoon was driven into the whale, the boat was pulled through the heavy seas by the infuriated animal until another sailor could kill it. There were numerous dangers involved in the chase, as can be seen in this passage from *Moby Dick*:

The harpoon was darted; the stricken whale flew forward; with igniting velocity the line ran through the groove;—ran foul. Ahab stooped to clear it; he did clear it; but the flying turn caught him round the neck, and voicelessly as Turkish mutes bowstring their victim, he was shot out of the boat, ere the crew knew he was gone. Next instant, the heavy eye-splice in the rope's final end flew out of the stark-empty tub, knocked down an oarsman, and smiting the sea, disappeared in its depths.

After many adventure-filled months at sea, the "Acushnet" dropped anchor in Anna Maria Bay, off the island of Nukuhiva. Beyond the beach rose mountains from which streams flowed into the ocean. Vine-covered cliffs guarded the harbor, and bamboo huts nestled close to the shore. Cannibals were said to live in the remote valleys of the island.

Melville later recalled in *Typee*: "Nothing can exceed the imposing scenery of this bay. Viewed from our ship as she lay at anchor in the middle of the harbour, it presented the appearance of a vast natural amphitheatre in decay, and overgrown with vines, the deep glens that furrowed its sides appearing like enormous fissures caused by the ravages of time."

Melville went ashore with other crew members. The lush tropical growth and exotic natives were so appealing that he decided to desert ship. Careful plans had to be laid, lest the captain be informed of his intentions. If Melville left the ship too soon, he could be captured and brought back in irons. A gun or bolt of cloth offered as reward to the natives would quickly bring about his capture.

The "Acushnet" lay at anchor in the bay for two weeks. This

gave Melville time to become familiar with the island and learn a few words of the native language. Before long he discovered that a shipmate named Toby Greene also planned to desert ship.

"I found him ripe for the enterprise," Melville wrote in *Typee*, "and a very few words sufficed for a mutual understanding between us. In an hour's time we had arranged all the preliminaries, and decided upon our plan of action . . . and, to elude suspicion, repaired each to his hammock, to spend the last night on board . . . ."

The crew were granted one more leave on the island before the "Acushnet" sailed. The deserters hid food under their clothing and went ashore with the other men. They slipped away during a rainstorm, climbed a mountain, and watched as their ship set sail. They had not been missed.

In *Typee*, Melville describes their first hours of freedom: ". . . we found ourselves, about three hours before sunset, standing on the top of what seemed to be the highest land on the island . . . . We must have been more than three thousand feet above the level of the sea, and the scenery viewed from this height was magnificent . . . and were I to live a hundred years, I should never forget the feeling of admiration which I then experienced."

But the coconuts and other tropical fruit they expected to find in abundance were not there; they found only a thick tangle of jungle growth in the low-lying areas, and a series of rocky chasms and crevices among the mountains, "deep recesses . . . damp and chill to a degree that one would hardly anticipate in such a climate . . . ."

Five days of aimless wandering through mountains and valleys produced only disappointment for Melville and Toby. Melville had wounded one of his legs early in the adventure; it became infected and made walking difficult. He was at times delirious. Toby's indomitable spirit was close to broken. At last they were faced with a decision: starve to death on a mountain or take their chances in the Valley of the Taipi-Vai, a people reportedly cannibalistic. When Melville later wrote his novel *Typee*, he changed this to the Valley of the Typee, the name used for this locality throughout this narrative.

Cautiously, Melville and Toby descended the mountain and entered the Valley of the Typee. "With what apprehensions we proceeded, ignorant at what moment we might be greeted by the javelin of some ambushed savage!" But they found the natives friendly and anxious to care for Melville's wounded leg.

Melville learned much about the culture of the Typee people during his sojourn in their valley. They were cannibals, but Toby and Melville found favor with them. Melville was initiated into secret rites known only to the men of Typee. They also shared with him their art of making tapa cloth from the bleached bark of the mulberry tree.

Weeks slid by unnoticed as Melville and Toby indulged in the pleasures of native life: the daily feasts and the swimming parties in the lagoon, where they watched "the natives . . . ducking beneath the surface in all directions—the young girls springing buoyantly into the air, and revealing their naked forms to the waist . . . ." But Melville's leg failed to respond to native remedies, and he and Toby made plans to leave the valley. But the Typees would not allow them to go. Finally, they agreed to allow Toby to go to Anna Maria Bay for medical aid. Upon arrival in the settlement, Toby was shanghaied and taken aboard a whaling vessel which had dropped anchor there; he was therefore unable to send help to his friend.

One day when Melville returned to the village home in which he had been a guest, he was horrified and sickened to find his host, Marheyo, and his family examining three human heads, one of them a white man's. After this shocking discovery, Melville naturally began to speculate upon his own fate among the Typees. The two days which followed were like a nightmare. The steady, thunderous beating of native drums pounded in his ears, and he was forbidden to approach or enter the Ti (men's house) or the Tabooed Groves. On the third day he was allowed to visit the Ti. Upon entering, Melville's glance fell on a carved wooden bowl, partially covered. It contained "the disordered members of a human skeleton, the bones still fresh with moisture . . . ."

By this time, another whaling ship, the "Lucy Ann," had dropped anchor off the island of Nukuhiva. News had spread throughout the island that an American was being held prisoner in Typee Valley. Upon hearing of this from friendly natives who came out to greet the "Lucy Ann," the captain sent a boat ashore. It reached the island just in time to rescue Melville, who had escaped from the valley minutes before the boat arrived.

Melville found the conditions aboard the "Lucy Ann" much worse than those on the "Acushnet." Serving under the "Acushnet" 's half-mad captain had been difficult. But where his former master had dominated the crew through fear, the captain of the "Lucy Ann" was unable to command any kind of respect from his crew. To make matters worse, he had become seriously ill and was forced to turn the command of his vessel over to the first mate, who was drunk more often than he was sober. When the "Lucy Ann" dropped anchor at Papeete, in the Tahitian Islands, the captain was taken ashore for medical treatment. But he would not allow any of the crew to leave the ship.

The crew, wild with anger and resentful of the cruel working and living conditions, broke into open rebellion. Melville and Long Ghost, the demoted surgeon of the "Lucy Ann," tried to steer the men into a more moderate course of action. But when the crew refused to listen to reason, Melville knew the situation was hopeless and joined the mutiny. The English authorities on Tahiti arrested the crew and placed them in jail.

The "Lucy Ann" sailed with another crew, shanghaied from the streets and beaches of Tahiti. Soon afterwards, Melville and the others were released from the jail and allowed to roam the island at will.

Melville and Long Ghost stayed on Tahiti for a month, then went to a neighboring island to work on a plantation. When a ship stopped there to take on fruit and fresh water, Melville joined its crew. He left Long Ghost on the island. "I have never seen or heard of him since," Melville recorded in *Omoo*. The ship was bound for Hawaii: "Once more the sailor's cradle rocked under me," he wrote, "and I found myself rolling in my gait. By noon, the island had gone down in the horizon; and all before us was the wide Pacific."

Melville left the ship at Honolulu and found work as a store clerk. When the American Navy's frigate "United States" dropped anchor in the harbor, Melville enlisted in the Navy for a year's cruise to end in Boston.

Melville found life aboard a warship much different from that on a whaling ship. For one thing, he had to sleep in a hammock instead of a bunk and store the hammock away each morning. The warship was larger and carried twenty times as many men as a whaling ship. When Melville was off duty, he had to seek out a small space into which he could squeeze to avoid being stepped upon by another man on duty. But if he was on duty in the morning, he could be free in the afternoon. This was very different from the fourteen hours of hard labor aboard the "St. Lawrence" and the eighteen or more on a whaling ship.

In good weather Melville joined other off-duty men on deck. Those who were not busy keeping journals of the cruise usually spent their off-duty time mending clothes, playing checkers, or gambling (though this was against ship's rules) while a lookout watched for officers who might be lurking nearby.

Grog was "served out just previous to breakfast and dinner," Melville wrote in *White-Jacket*.

At the roll of the drum, the sailors assemble round a large tub, or cask, filled with the liquid; and, as their names are called off by a midshipman, they step up and regale themselves from a little tin measure called a "tot." . . . To many of them, indeed, the thought of their daily tots forms a perpetual perspective of ravishing land-scapes, indefinitely receding in the distance. It is their great "pros-pect in life." Take away their grog, and life possesses no further charms for them.

Next to mutiny, the most chaotic situation that could occur aboard a navy sailing vessel in Melville's time was for it to run out of grog.

Melville reached Boston on October 14, 1844, almost five years after he had sailed for the South Seas aboard the "Acush-net." He had seen more adventure than he had dreamed existed a few years before when he read *Two Years Before the Mast.*

Upon Melville's return, he discovered that South Sea stories were still popular among readers. He realized that the time was right for a book about his adventures on Nukuhiva. At the urg-ing of family and friends, he wrote the novel *Typee*, published in 1846, soon to be followed by a sequel, *Omoo*, in 1847. Walt Whitman, then editor of the *Brooklyn Eagle*, said of *Typee*: "It is a strange, graceful, most readable book."

Many readers did not believe the adventures described in *Typee* to be true. Melville became concerned lest his career as an author be damaged by adverse public opinion. But Toby Greene, his companion in the Typee Valley adventure, reap-peared at just the right moment and stated that he was "happy to testify to the entire accuracy of the work." The public was re-assured and Melville's reputation as a writer saved.

As the author of a successful novel, Melville's name was al-most a household word. His fame, added to the fact that he was a handsome young bachelor, suggests that he could have en-joyed the attention of numerous young ladies. But Herman's nature was extremely retiring where women were concerned, and such adulation held little appeal for him. In the summer of 1847, shortly before the publication of *Omoo*, he married Miss Elizabeth Shaw of Boston, whom he had known from childhood. Her father, Judge Lemuel Shaw, Chief Justice of Massachusetts, and Melville's parents had been friends from youth. After Allan Melville's death, Judge Shaw had often come to the aid of the impoverished family. The relationship of Herman and "Lizzie" had, until their marriage, been more that of cousins than romantic lovers. Although their lives together as husband and wife were not to be distinguished by an exceptional romantic or intellectual attraction, Lizzie's devotion to making her husband's many years of creative and financial difficulties more comfortable was tender and constant.

The newlyweds moved into a house in New York City—shared with Melville's younger brother Allan, Allan's wife Maria, and Allan's and Herman's four unmarried sisters. Herman and Lizzie had two rooms to themselves.

The household routine, as finally agreed upon, permitted Melville six uninterrupted hours a day for writing. The family had breakfast together at eight, after which Melville took a walk while Lizzie straightened out their rooms. This allowed four quiet hours for work before lunch. After lunch he took another walk, this time with Lizzie. Then he wrote until the dinner bell sounded.

In the evening he sometimes read the day's composition to Lizzie or walked downtown for a glance at the newspapers in a public reading room, later joining his wife and the family for cards and conversation in the living room. By adhering to this schedule, Melville completed three books in less than a year: *Mardi*, *Redburn*, and *White-Jacket*.

It was also at this time, the winter of 1849, that Melville began a thorough reading of William Shakespeare's plays. "Ah, he's full of sermons-on-the-mount," he wrote, "and gentle, aye, almost as Jesus." The concentration with which Melville read Shakespeare is apparent from his pencil markings in the volumes of his set of the Bard's works, now preserved in the Harvard College Library. These markings are heaviest in *Antony and Cleopatra* and *King Lear*. Melville once expressed to a friend the wish that Shakespeare might have been his contemporary, so that "the muzzle which all men wore on their souls in the Elizabethan day, might not have intercepted . . . [his] free articulations."

Through his study of Shakespeare, Melville entered a new realm of creativity. He was now a man of thirty and the author of five best-selling novels, but the full awakening of his creative capacities was still to come. As he pondered the meaning of Shakespeare's plays, his own work in turn was released from limited confines of mere reporting to the expression of deeper, more profound concepts. Thus his writing gained force from Shakespeare, but still was based on man and nature as only he, Melville, knew them.

Melville was physically and mentally exhausted by the end of the summer of 1849. He went to England in October to rest and to investigate the possibility of having *White-Jacket* published there. His first night at sea brought back memories of his voyages. He climbed the masthead and felt again the exhilaration of the wind whipping about his clothing and face. Yet he was lonely for Lizzie and their infant son Malcolm.

Refreshed and anxious to begin work on a new book after his return from England, Melville settled down to plan and write *Moby Dick*. Shortly after he began this book, he moved his family to Arrowhead Farm, near Pittsfield, Massachusetts, for he needed the quiet atmosphere of the country in which to work. He grew enough food for his family's needs, and it was not long before there was enough produce to spare for the market; thus he received a small unexpected income.

It took Melville a little more than a year to complete *Moby Dick*, which was published in the fall of 1851. His primary design for this monumental novel was to endow the whaling industry with a mythology befitting the fundamental struggle between man and nature and to "dive into the souls" of men, even if that meant "to bring up mud from the bottom." While he was still working strenuously to finish the closing chapter, the first chapters were already being driven through the press.

But the critics, who had been so enthusiastic in their praise of *Typee* and *Omoo*, received *Moby Dick* coldly. One of them even called it "so much trash belonging to the worst school of Bedlam literature." Not until after Melville's death would readers discover the true greatness of this work.

"Dollars damn me," Melville brooded in a letter to his close friend Nathaniel Hawthorne. "What I feel most moved to write, that is banned,—it will not pay. Yet, altogether, write the *other* way I cannot. So the product is a final hash, and all my books are botches."

That the creation and production of *Moby Dick* had taken much out of him artistically was clearly evident the following year when he wrote *Pierre*, an inferior piece of work by comparison. His next two novels *Israel Potter* and *The Confidence Man* were also poorly written, though they earned a small amount of success.

Melville could no longer satisfy himself by writing for popular tastes, and his inspiration seemed depleted. Desperately, his family urged him to go on a tour of the Holy Land, hoping that such a tour would renew his creative energy and provide him with fresh ideas. The trip did result in the long poem *Clarel*, but that was not published until 1876, nineteen years after his return.

Melville was mildly successful as a lecturer during this period, and like Walt Whitman, he visited the battle lines in Virginia at the time of the Civil War. Unlike Whitman, however, Melville took no active role in the war. But after the war, he wrote a collection of poems which formed a historic portrayal of the conflict. In spite of their suitability to the period, Melville had difficulty finding a publisher for them. *Battle Pieces and Aspects of the War* did not appear in print until 1866. In the supplement to this book he wrote prophetically:

. . . we should remember that emancipation was accomplished not by deliberate legislation; only through agonized violence could so mighty a result be effected. In our natural solicitude to confirm the benefit of liberty to the blacks, let us forbear from measures of dubious constitutional rightfulness toward our white countrymen—measures of a nature to provoke, among other of the last evils, exterminating hatred of race toward race. In imagination let us place ourselves in the unprecedented position of the Southerners . . . . Let us be Christians toward our fellow-whites, as well as philanthropists toward the blacks, our fellow-men.

After the close of the war, Melville sold Arrowhead Farm to his brother Allan and moved back to New York City. Although he was only forty-seven years old, he seemed an old man. His career as an author appeared to be ended. His early novels still sold well, but the income from them was not enough to support his family, which now included four children.

In 1866, through political appointment, Melville secured a post as Deputy Inspector of Customs for the Port of New York City. Few people outside his family and close friends knew of his position at the Customs House. When he was not on duty, he spent his time writing or puttering in his rose garden, but he published nothing during this period. In 1882, he was invited to assist in the founding of the Author's Club in New York City, but he refused the honor. In short, Herman Melville, author of *Typee*, *Omoo*, and *Moby Dick*, preferred to be forgotten.

It was not until after Melville retired from the Customs House in 1885 that he again gave serious thought to writing for publication. These quiet years had produced numerous incomplete manuscripts, most of them scribbled on small slips of paper which he carried in his coat pocket. *John Marr and Other Sailors*, a volume of sea poems, evolved from these scraps.

Another novel was yet to flow from Melville's pen. "In this matter of writing," he announced, "resolve as one may to keep to the main road, some by-paths have an enticement not readily to be withstood. Beckoned by the genius of Nelson, I am going to err into such a by-path. . . ." The result was *Billy Budd, Foretopman*, based on the recollections of Melville's cousin, Guert

Gansevoort. As a young naval officer half a century earlier, Gansevoort had taken part in the court-martial of a sailor charged with mutiny. The sailor had been found guilty and hanged from the yard-arm of his ship; later he was proved innocent and a victim of injustice. Now the case came again to the public's attention through a magazine article. Melville's early knowledge of the incident had been intimate because of his cousin's participation; and although thirty years had passed since he had written a full-length book of prose, his imagination was reawakened by the article.

Shortly before his death on September 28, 1891, Melville finished *Billy Budd, Foretopman*, his last novel. The manuscript was left in a very rough condition, and it was not edited and published until 1924. It had been discovered in an old tin box several years earlier, along with a number of Melville's unpublished poems. Although Melville had slipped away quietly, neither mourned nor missed by the public, the publication of this short novel marked the beginning of a revival of interest in every detail of his life and work.

Suggested Reading*

NOVELS AND POETRY BY HERMAN MELVILLE:

Battle-Pieces of Herman Melville, The. Edited with Introduction and Notes by Hennig Cohen. New York: Thomas Yoseloff, 1964.

Billy Budd. New York: AMSCO School Publications, 1969.

Clarel. Edited by Walter E. Bezanson. New York: Hendricks House, 1959.

Collected Poems (except *Clarel*). Edited by Howard P. Vincent. New York: Hendricks House, 1946.

Confidence Man, The. Bridgeport, Conn.: Airmont Publishing Co.†

Five Tales. Great Illus. Classics. New York: Dodd, Mead & Co., 1967.

Four Short Novels. New York: Bantam Books, 1971.

Mardi. Edited by Tyrus Hillway. Masterworks of Literature Series. New Haven, Conn.: College & University Press, 1972.

Moby-Dick. New York: The Macmillan Co., 1962.

Omoo. New York: Hendricks House.†

Piazza Tales. Edited by Egbert S. Oliver. New York: Hendricks House, 1962.

Pierre. The Writings of Herman Melville Series. Evanston, Ill.: Northwestern University Press, 1971.

Redburn. New York: Doubleday & Co., 1957.

Typee. New York: Bantam Books, 1958.

White-Jacket. New York: Holt, Rinehart & Winston, 1948.

BOOKS ABOUT HERMAN MELVILLE:

Cantwell, Robert. "Herman Melville," *Famous Men of Letters.* New York: Dodd, Mead & Co., 1956.

Gould, Jean Rosalind. *Young Mariner Melville.* Illus. by Donald McKay. New York: Dodd, Mead & Co., 1956.

Hough, Henry Beetle. *Melville in the South Pacific.* Illus. by Frank Nicholas. Boston: Houghton Mifflin Co., 1960.

Keyes, Charlotte E. *High on the Mainmast: The Life of Herman Melville.* New Haven, Conn.: College & University Press, 1966.

Lockerbie, D. Bruce. *Melville.* New York: Holt, Rinehart & Winston, 1966.

* The author has listed popular editions for convenient reference.
† Publication date not available.

Walt Whitman

Walt Whitman
/He Heard America Singing

Walter Whitman, Sr., was a stubborn man. He had chosen the worst possible day to move his family from the Long Island countryside to the village of Brooklyn, New York: May 27, 1823. The highway was always dusty and by this time of the year often unbearably warm. Today it was also jammed with horses and carriages. The reason: There was to be a race that day at Jamaica, Long Island, between Eclipse, the most famous racehorse in the North, and Henry, the fastest horse in the South, and people were flocking from New York City to see the race. The Whitmans' wagon, overloaded with children, pets, and household goods and trailing a cow behind it, could barely move through the traffic.

This was an exciting day for little Walter, but only the first of many changes to take place throughout his life. He had been born in West Hills, Long Island, on May 31, 1819. His father was a carpenter and was now moving the family to Brooklyn because there was no longer enough work for him on Long Island.

Later that afternoon, when the Whitmans had arrived at their new home, young Walter watched the stagecoaches and carriages returning from Jamaica. The ferry landing was close to the Whitman house, and from the front yard Walter could see the happy crowds waiting for the boat to take them across the river to the city. Eclipse had won the race!

At that time, there was no bridge across the East River from New York City to Brooklyn, which was then a rural community.

The Whitmans' new home was not far from the United States Navy Yard, the only substantial sign of progress in the area. No city conveniences existed, such as paved (cobblestone) streets. The streets were mudholes from one end to the other and were littered with garbage thrown there by local residents careless in their sanitary habits. Pigs, which ran loose in the community, rooted through the refuse. Pedestrians never walked too close to buildings more than one story high because housewives were not choosy about what direction the wind happened to be blowing when they emptied their slop jars from second-story windows.

Most of the people who lived in this section of Brooklyn were day laborers. They were crude, uneducated, and brashly ignorant. This was a jungle-like existence in which only the very strong survived physically, and few ever rose above their surroundings intellectually. There might as well have been no laws. Crime was unchecked because there was no police force. A Sunday school movement had been started in 1815 to help combat crime among children, as well as to teach reading and writing to the many who received no other formal education.

For Walter, the change from the quiet, clean life of a Long Island farm to Brooklyn, which appeared to revel in its filth and disorder, could have been tragic had he not been blessed with the placid disposition of his Dutch ancestors. He contrasted with the children into whose midst he was thrown. Many were the offspring of immigrants who knew little English and had even less money than the Whitmans. There were better neighborhoods to be found on the outskirts of the village, but Walter's father could not afford to buy a house at this time, or to pay rent in a more respectable section.

Young Walter was fortunate in that throughout his formative years he remained untouched by the instinctive cruelty, hate, dishonesty, and greed that colored the thinking of those among whom he grew up. As he developed, he appeared set apart even from his brothers and sisters, all of whom were of a practical turn of mind. He was more strongly influenced by his father than were the other children in the family.

Although Walter Whitman, Sr., earned his living with his hands, he possessed an inquiring mind. He read broadly and attended the numerous lectures which were popular in New York City during the early 1800's. Young Walter learned to enjoy reading partly because his father disapproved of any entertainment more boisterous than that in the house. And his father was a man easily roused to anger.

The senior Whitman quickly found work in Brooklyn and before long became a building contractor. His practice was to build a house, move his family into it, and live there until he sold it. Then he would move into another house he was building which was close to completion. Unsettled as this life appeared, it eventually enabled the family to move into better neighborhoods.

When Walter was six years old, the village of Brooklyn built a new library. General Lafayette, "the old companion of Washington," was visiting America at the time, and he agreed to lay the cornerstone for the new building. The townspeople were thrilled at the prospect of the General's visit. A ceremony was planned for the Fourth of July.

Together with the mayor, the Revolutionary War veterans, and other important citizens, the schoolchildren marched from the ferryboat landing, where they greeted the General, to the building site. They paraded through the village, with Lafayette riding in a yellow coach and waving his hat to the crowd. When the parade reached its destination, the men in the crowd lifted the younger children to a place where they could see the activities. Lafayette helped move the children. He picked up the six-year-old Walter Whitman, pressed him for a moment to his breast, gave him a kiss, and handed him down to a safe spot in the excavation. Whitman later wrote in his book of reminiscent prose, *Specimen Days:* "I yet remember Lafayette's visit."

Although in later years Whitman's learning was great, his actual formal education was brief. He attended public school for only six years, and the conditions under which he studied make his intellectual development seem an even greater phenomenon. It was not unusual for one teacher, assisted by several older students, to have as many as three hundred children in one class, which was divided among several rooms. Ten children were often seated at each desk.

The teacher was sometimes not very well grounded in the basics of education because intellectually competent men and women often would not enter the teaching profession; the pay was poor and the working conditions deplorable. There was little opportunity for the student to express his individuality in such a school. The student assistants, most of whom were themselves dull and unimaginative, were first taught the lessons by the teacher in charge. They, in turn, instructed the students in arithmetic, geography, reading, and writing.

The possibility that a child with Walter's creative abilities, which may have been evident even at this early age, would be recognized and encouraged was nonexistent. Since discipline was rigidly enforced, any child who varied even slightly from the rules laid down by the teacher would have been punished by the student assistant in charge of that room. Even a show of individuality or imagination would have been defined as disobedience and rewarded by physical punishment. The only known record of Walter's conduct at school testified that his teachers thought him slovenly in appearance.

When Walter was not in school, he was often at the seashore on Long Island. He loved the ocean. In the winter he would cut holes in the ice of Long Island Sound and spear eels; on summer days he gathered sea gulls' eggs on the sandy shore and dug for clams. He enjoyed sailing and took walking trips around the island, making friends with herdsmen, farmers, and fishermen. Walter felt comfortable with these simple folk and they with him.

When he was eleven years old, Walter left school and went to work as an office boy in a law firm. The men for whom he worked were interested enough in his future to help him improve his handwriting and composition. One of his duties in the law office was to take messages across the river to Aaron Burr, who lived in New Jersey. Whitman in later years remembered Burr as "very gentle." "He had a way of giving me a bit of fruit on these visits—an apple or a pear. I can see him clearly, still—his stateliness, gray hair, courtesy, consideration," he remarked to a biographer.

At the end of two years Walter left the law office and became apprentice to the editor of the *Long Island Patriot*. The *Patriot*, published on Long Island and distributed in Brooklyn, was designed to appeal to Brooklyn's population of mechanics, laborers, and artisans, "off-spring of ignorant and poor, boys apprenticed to trades." One of the *Patriot*'s mottoes, prominently displayed on its masthead, was "the right of the people to rule in every case." This philosophy agreed with Whitman's budding idealism. He possessed an innate sympathy for people of the working class, and this interest expressed itself in short articles he contributed to the newspaper.

On Sundays Walter often took the ferry to New York City, "Superb-faced Manhattan! / . . . Where our tall-topt marble and iron beauties range on opposite sides . . . ." The city was a more exciting place for a young man than Brooklyn or Long Island.

On one of his expeditions to the city, Walter saw John Jacob Astor, the financier, "a bent, feeble but stout-built very old man, bearded, swathed in rich furs, with a great ermine cap on his head, led and assisted, almost carried, down the steps of his high front stoop . . . and then lifted and tuck'd in a gorgeous sleigh, envelop'd in other furs, for a ride."

Another of Walter's favorite entertainments was the theatre. "I frequented the old Park, the Bowery, Broadway and Chatham-square theatres," he wrote in *Specimen Days*. "What names, reminiscences, the words bring back!"

When Walter was sixteen, he completed his apprenticeship in the newspaper office and became a journeyman printer. He worked as a compositor for a newspaper in New York City and lived in a boarding house. Around him the great restless city was bulging with an overflow of Irish immigrants. New York was their landing place, and many chose to remain in the city to work.

During the summer of 1835 a brutal riot between these immigrants and a group of resentful Americans broke out in the Bowery Theatre. It was only one of many such clashes. Citizens were forced to avoid certain sections of the city day and night and to remain at home as much as possible.

Whitman was directly affected by the unrest in the city when uncontrollable fires broke out as a result of one of these riots and destroyed the printing district. The young journeyman printer was out of work and had no choice but to return to the family roof. By now, land prices in Brooklyn had risen so high that building had practically come to a halt, and the senior Whitman had been forced to give up his construction business and return to farming.

As a temporary means of support, Walter took a post as schoolteacher on Long Island, though the salary was much less than what he could earn as a printer. The schoolhouse was a one-room building with an open fireplace for heat. This was an uncomfortable arrangement for students and teacher alike: Those who sat close to the fire were always too warm, while those in the back of the room were never warm enough. Thus there was a constant shifting around that disrupted order in the classroom.

Walter was a conscientious teacher and gave special attention to the younger students. He never punished a student by whipping him but always sought a constructive correction to disobedience. If he caught a student lying, for instance, he rebuked him by telling the class a story in a way that allowed the prevaricating student to get the point without being called by name.

In the spring of 1838, Walter gave up schoolteaching and started a weekly newspaper called the *Long Islander*. He did most of the work himself, with the assistance of his brother George. The two brothers lived in a room over the newspaper office, and their friends often gathered there in the evening for cards and conversation.

Walter was moderate in his personal habits and never smoked or drank. He did not appear to have a serious interest in young women, though it has been said that he had a sweetheart. As if to protect himself from the speculative theories of future biographers, Whitman, in his old age, confided to a friend that he had fathered six illegitimate children. But he admitted that he was as strongly attracted to men as to women. Some writers, commenting on this complexity of his nature, point to his "Calamus" poems as his own admission of homosexuality. Other writers say that his "Children of Adam" poems testify to a normal relationship with women. One biographer has claimed that he may have been bisexual.

After he gave up his newspaper on Long Island, Whitman became editor of a small daily newspaper in New York City. In his column he defended Charles Dickens who, during his visit to America in 1842, complained that although his books were being published in this country, he was not receiving any royalties from the sales. Dickens' critical attitude toward the United States while on this tour had already aroused a strong distaste for him and his books among the American people. Whitman's defense of the Englishman was, therefore, poorly timed, and he was fired from his editorial post. But the *Brooklyn Eagle* was quick to hire the now controversial young journalist.

As editor of the *Eagle*, Whitman led crusades for any and all good causes. He opposed war; he cheered the popular issue of equal rights and higher pay for women; and he wrote often on the subject of music, stressing the appeal of folk-singing and the Italian opera. "This musical passion follow'd my theatrical one," he recorded in *Specimen Days*. It was Whitman's dream that music be taught as a regular subject in the public schools.

In 1848 when Whitman was invited to edit a daily newspaper

in New Orleans, he and his brother Jeff "went off on a leisurely journey and working expedition...through all the middle States, and down the Ohio and Mississippi rivers." This was Whitman's first opportunity to see the country outside of the New York City area and to "dwell a while in every city and town." The brothers departed from New York City on a train, transferred to a stage-coach, and then boarded a Mississippi riverboat. The boat served mainly as a river freighter and carried only a few passengers. It stopped at plantation ports, or stations, along the way to take on produce and sometimes to discharge freight brought down the river from northern cities.

Whitman's impressions of the country broadened and deep-ened from these travels. Never before had he understood so clearly the vast potentials inherent in this great land: the room for expansion and development of cities, farmland, and industry, and the growth of population westward. What he observed ex-cited him to wonderful visions and stirred his poetic imagination to sing:

> Chants of the prairies,
> Chants of the long-running Mississippi, and down to the
>   Mexican sea,
> Chants of Ohio, Indiana, Illinois, Iowa, Wisconsin and
>   Minnesota,
> Chants going forth from the centre from Kansas, and thence
>   equidistant,
> Shooting in pulses of fire ceaseless to vivify all.

The year 1850 marked a dramatic change in Whitman's ap-pearance and personality. Until this date, he seemed to be an average young man equipped with a normal ambition to succeed in his chosen field of work, that of printing and writing. He did not burn with ambition in any particular direction, unless his political views were stirred. Even this motivation was not great enough for him to take an aggressive step, such as to run for office.

Whitman supported the political interests of the common man: the laborer, the mechanic, the skilled and unskilled worker. He wrote about his beliefs in the columns of the newspapers for which he worked and on occasion made a fiery political speech. Otherwise, he did not outshine any of his young fellow-journalists. His dress was conventional, and his tastes in entertainment, such as opera and the theatre, were those of every other intellectual of his day.

In 1850, Whitman was thirty-one years old. Two years earlier he had worked in New Orleans as an editor. This three-month period away from home, the longest he had ever spent separated from his family (except for his brother Jeff, who was with him), may have given him a new view of himself. He doffed his conservative coat, collar, and tie for the rough clothing of a day laborer or mechanic. His shirt was artfully left open at the neck to reveal a red undershirt, and his trousers were worn loose, tucked into high-laced boots. He sported a rakish felt hat with a wide brim, and his beard, which had already begun to turn gray, gave a final touch to his carefully created image of the working man's champion. All that remained to be changed was his reserved manner, which soon yielded to a spirit of camaraderie. Walter Whitman, printer and journalist, was preparing to become Walt Whitman, poet.

Upon his return to Brooklyn, Walt helped his father build a new home for the family. He used the first floor of the house as a printing office and for a short time published *The Freeman*. Originally a weekly newspaper, it became a daily. Although he could have found another editorial post in New York City or Brooklyn, Walt chose to run his printshop and work with his father as a carpenter until the elder Whitman's death in 1855.

Working with his hands gave Walt a feeling of being closer to mankind and to nature, though he was too slow a worker to depend upon carpentry for his living.

For pleasure Whitman returned to his old pastime of riding ferryboats and observing "the shipping of Manhattan north and

west, and the heights of Brooklyn to the south and east." He also
liked to ride up Broadway on top of a horse-drawn double-decker
bus, from which he could see "million-footed Manhattan un-
pent." Whitman described these jaunts in *Specimen Days*:

How many hours, forenoons and afternoons—how many exhilarating
night-times I have had . . . riding the whole length of Broadway,
listening to some yarn . . . or perhaps I declaiming some stormy
passage from Julius Caesar or Richard, (you could roar as loudly as
you chose in that heavy, dense, uninterrupted street-bass.) Yes, I
knew all the drivers then . . . . They had immense qualities . . . . Not
only for comradeship . . . great studies I found them also.

Once, when a driver was sick, Whitman took his place until
the man was well enough to return to work. Then he collected
the driver's wages and took them to the man and his family,
who were in greater need of the money than he.

When Walt was not working at carpentry, he appeared to be
loafing. But idly reading or observing the vast cross-section of
humanity even then centered in New York City was his relaxed
approach to learning. Writing of this period in his life, Whitman
reflected:

. . . I used to go off, sometimes for a week at a stretch, down in the
country, or to Long Island's seashores—there, in the presence of outdoor influences, I went over thoroughly the Old and New Testa-
ments, and absorb'd (probably to better advantage for me than in
any library or indoor room—it makes such difference *where* you
read,) Shakspere, Ossian, the best translated versions I could get
of Homer, Eschylus, Sophocles, the old German Nibelungen, the
ancient Hindoo poems, and one or two other masterpieces, Dante's
among them.

In 1855, Whitman gave up the carpentry trade and devoted
all his time to the completion and printing of *Leaves of Grass*.
He had become an increasing problem to his family during the
five years since he had given up editorial work. He slept late
almost every morning and never said when he was going out or

what time he would return home. If dinner was served at one o'clock, he might come home at three. All the other men in the family lived at home and worked at regular jobs, and they considered Walt thoughtless, lazy, and selfish. It would have been impossible for them to understand that he had a greater purpose in life than the carpentry trade or the earning of daily wages; that he was to evolve into one of the giants of American literature, becoming the father of modern American poetry, the innovator of a new verse form. As he himself explained in the Preface of the first edition of *Leaves of Grass*, published in 1855, he was to be one who "sees the solid and beautiful forms of the future where there are now no solid forms."

Each day when he set out to work in the carpentry trade with his father and brothers, Walt took with him a book to read during the lunch hour. His selection of a volume from his own meagre library, or the local lending library, was casual. He merely wanted something to divert and lift his thought from the daily work routine. But one day he happened to tuck a volume of Ralph Waldo Emerson's essays into his lunch pail, and while he was browsing through the essay titled "The Poet," a light suddenly turned on in Walt's consciousness. He later wrote: "I was simmering, simmering, simmering; Emerson brought me to a boil."

Whitman had read Emerson's essays many times before, but this was a special day. It was the beginning of a totally new concept in Whitman's writing experience—and in American poetry. It was the day modern American poetry was born:

> Out of the cradle endlessly rocking,
> Out of the mocking-bird's throat, the musical shuttle,
> Out of the Ninth-month midnight . . . .

As early as 1847 Whitman had recorded in a notebook that "a man is only interested in anything when he identifies himself with it." This is a brief though concise description of the substance of his poetry. The opening lines of the first poem in the 1855 edition of his book offer a clear illustration of this point. In this poem, titled "Song of Myself," Whitman startled his staid Victorian readers with the blatant declaration:

I celebrate myself, and sing myself,
And what I assume you shall assume,
For every atom belonging to me as good belongs to you.

Whitman told a friend and biographer, "Remember, the book arose out of my life in Brooklyn and New York from 1838 to 1853, absorbing a million people, for fifteen years with an intimacy, an eagerness, an abandon probably never equalled." His use of words was new, fresh, almost childlike. One biographer has written: "His book broke all the rules. For one thing, his lines did not rhyme. They were almost as formless as prose. While the established American poets were writing verse fit for the albums on parlor tables Walt was sending his barbaric *yawp* over the roofs of the world." Another critic has claimed that Whitman's language was more earthy than that of other poets of the period because he was conscious of the power of sex in literature. For a generation of readers who had not yet brought itself to admit that ladies possessed "legs" instead of "limbs," this was a stunning jolt into reality.

Whitman printed his book in the printing office of friends, "the brothers Rome, in Brooklyn." He set the type and operated the press himself. When he brought the first copies home, his family looked upon his accomplishment with little interest. George Whitman's comment was: "I saw the book but did not read it at all. Didn't think it was worth reading." Whitman's mother, a loving but relatively uneducated woman, read it but confessed that she did not understand it.

Although Whitman's family failed to comprehend the value of his book, *Leaves of Grass* received praise from several respected writers in America. Ralph Waldo Emerson wrote Whitman a letter, thanking him for the copy he had sent, and later called on the youthful poet at his home, as did Henry Thoreau. Emerson was generous in praise of *Leaves of Grass* in his first letter to Whitman:

I am not blind to the worth of the wonderful gift of "Leaves of Grass." I find it the most extraordinary piece of wit and wisdom that America has yet contributed. . . . I greet you at the beginning of a great career, which yet must have had a long foreground somewhere, for such a start. I rubbed my eyes a little to see if this sunbeam were no illusion; but the solid sense of the book is a sober certainty. It has the best merits, namely, of fortifying and encouraging.

Another copy of *Leaves of Grass* found its way to a table in the law office of Abraham Lincoln in Springfield, Illinois. Lincoln read it thoughtfully and was delighted with the fresh new form of composition. It is reported that he ordered the book to be left on the table and often read aloud from it. But Whitman did not at first return the admiration. When Lincoln won the presidential election of 1860, the poet had little faith in his ability to head the government. Later, during the Civil War, Whitman did become a great admirer of the President.

The impact of the secession of the southern states from the Union in 1861 was graphically recorded by Whitman in *Specimen Days:*

News of the attack on Fort Sumter and *the flag* at Charleston harbor, S.C., was receiv'd in New York city late at night . . . and was immediately sent out in extras of the newspapers. I had been to the opera in Fourteenth street that night, and after the performance was walking down Broadway toward twelve o'clock, on my way to Brooklyn, when I heard in the distance the loud cries of the newsboys, who came presently tearing and yelling up the street, rushing from side to side even more furiously than usual. I bought an extra and cross'd to the Metropolitan hotel (Niblo's) where the great lamps were still brightly blazing, and, with a crowd of others, who gather'd impromptu, read the news, which was evidently authentic. For the benefit of some who had no papers, one of us read the telegram aloud, while all listen'd silently and attentively. No remark was made by any of the crowd, which had increas'd to thirty or forty, but all stood a minute or two, I remember, before they dispers'd. I can almost see them there now, under the lamps at midnight again.

Walter's brother George immediately enlisted in the Union Army as a lieutenant. Since Walt was now the oldest son at home, he remained to support his mother and invalid brother, Edward. But when George was wounded in the Virginia campaign, Walter felt it necessary to go to his side in Virginia. After George's recovery, Walter stopped in Washington, D.C., on his way back to Brooklyn, to visit the wounded soldiers. His deep sympathy for these men made him decide to stay and help in the hospitals. He wrote:

My place in Washington was a peculiar one; my reasons for being there; my doing there what I did do. I do not think I quite had my match. People went there for all sorts of reasons, none of which were my reasons . . . .

But no one—at least no one I met—went just from my own reasons, from a profound conviction of necessity, affinity, coming into closest relations—relations O so close and dear!—with the whole strange welter of life gathered to that mad focus. . . .

It was in such an experience as of the war that my heart needed to be fully thrown—thrown without reserve. I do not regret it—could not regret it. What was a man to do? The war had much to give— there were thousands, tens of thousands, hundreds of thousands needing me—needing all who might come. What could I do?

Whitman needed money, not only to support himself but also to help carry on his work. He therefore took a job as a copyist in the Paymaster's Office. The work took only three hours a day, after which he visited the hospitals. When Whitman's friends heard of his activities in Washington, they sent money to help him continue and expand them. With this money, added to the little he earned, he bought fruit, books, candy, and other items he knew the men needed or would enjoy. Walt understood what pleasure and uplift of spirit even small gifts bring to men in hospitals. He was always careful to fit the gift to the man and overlooked no one, not even the wounded Confederate prisoners.

He moved among the wards, stopping to talk with the men and write letters for them. "I adapt myself to each case and to temperaments—some need to be humored; some are rather out of their head; some merely want me to sit with them and hold them by the hand." Noting the shortage of doctors and nurses, Whitman volunteered to learn how to dress wounds and nurse the suffering. He often sat up all night with a man in need. It was during these long hours that such lines as the following from "The Wound-Dresser" were inspired:

An old man bending I come among new faces . . . .
Bearing the bandages, water and sponge,
Straight and swift to my wounded I go,
Where they lie on the ground after the battle brought in . . . .
I am faithful, I do not give out . . . .

The "wound-dresser" spent little money for his own needs in order to have as much as possible for his hospital work, plus enough to send home to his mother and sick brother Edward. He lived in an attic room, bare except for a bed, a pine table, a little iron stove, and a few straight-backed chairs. He lit the stove only for cooking—wood cost money. The room remained unheated otherwise, and the windows were always open, even in winter.

Whitman's meals were simple. For breakfast he cut slices of bread with his jackknife and toasted them over the fire on a stick. He brewed tea in a tin kettle and spooned sugar from a brown paper bag. Another piece of brown paper served as a butter plate. A wooden box pushed against one wall was his cupboard, and his housekeeping utensils consisted of a tin cup, a bowl, and a spoon. But Whitman shared even these simple meals. "I have given a Michigan soldier his breakfast with me," he wrote in a letter to his mother. "He relished it, too . . . ."

When Whitman was not visiting hospitals or working in the Paymaster's Office, he roamed the streets of Washington in search of lonely, discouraged men. Confederate soldiers, weary of battle and burdened by a hopeless cause, sometimes crossed Union lines and came into Washington. Their clothes were tattered, their minds and bodies exhausted, their stomachs empty. Whitman sought out these men. He talked with them, gave them money, and directed them to friendly doors. Referring to the many opportunities he found to assist men in need, Whitman commented: "Another thing became clear to me—while *cash* is not amiss to bring up the rear, tact and magnetic sympathy and unction are, and ever will be, sovereign still."

During the war years, Whitman had become a staunch admirer and supporter of Abraham Lincoln. After Lincoln's assassination, he composed what has been claimed to be his most eloquent poem, "When Lilacs Last in the Dooryard Bloom'd." The poet's feeling of personal loss found further expression in "O Captain! My Captain!" in which he mourned:

My Captain does not answer, his lips are pale and still,
My father does not feel my arm, he has no pulse nor will,
The ship is anchor'd safe and sound, its voyage closed and done,
From fearful trip the victor ship comes in with object won . . . .

These two poems were included in *Drum Taps*, a small collection of poems describing Whitman's wartime experiences in Washington. This book was later incorporated into *Leaves of Grass*.

Although the fever pitch of Whitman's poetic activity declined after 1865, his fame continued to spread. A book of his selected poems was published in England in 1868. It received much higher and more widespread praise than his work had drawn in America. Poems were dedicated to him by English and European poets, and the literary community of England begged him to come there to live. But he preferred to stay in Washington, where he had been given a government post.

In 1873, Whitman was stricken with a paralysis that incapacitated him for the remaining nineteen years of his life. This marked the end of his active career, but he continued to write and publish poems and to revise and add to *Leaves of Grass*; eventually he included all his poems in this volume.

He was undecided now as to where to settle; his family in Brooklyn had either died or moved to other sections of the country. So, for a few years, he lived with his brother George in Camden, New Jersey. In 1884 Whitman bought a small two-story frame house on Mickle Street in Camden. This house was the "Good Gray Poet's" home for the last years of his life. It was close to the railroad in a poor neighborhood blanketed by smoke and soot from the steam engines and polluted by the smell of a fertilizer factory on the Delaware River. But Whitman was satisfied; there was a lilac bush in the back yard, and the streetcar to the Philadelphia ferry was one block away. He had many friends in the City of Brotherly Love.

As it became more difficult for Whitman to move about, his friends found a way to assist him. They presented him with a small carriage drawn by a pony named Frank. The pony was thought safe for the aging poet because it had been used to pull a cart for women and children at a nearby beach resort. But Whitman sold Frank and bought a more spirited horse. When asked what had become of the pony, Whitman replied, "He was groggy in the knees and too slow."

At Mickle Street, Whitman welcomed visitors from all corners of America and Europe. In 1888 the poet's devoted friend and aide, Horace Traubel, began making a voluminous verbatim record of their conversations, published later as *With Walt*

Whitman in Camden. Traubel visited Whitman two or three times a day during this period and later became one of his literary executors.

In his late years Whitman was painted, sculpted, and photographed more than any previous American author. On one occasion an English portrait artist and an American sculptor both asked permission to do his likeness at the same time. There was not enough space in the small parlor of Whitman's home to accommodate both artists at once, so the sculptor was persuaded to move his equipment to the back yard to allow the painter to set up his easel in the parlor, where Whitman sat. After many trips from the back yard, the sculptor completed his head of Whitman.

Whitman died on March 26, 1892. A year before, he had completed a series of short poems entitled *Good-bye My Fancy.* In a footnote to the title poem, he reflected:

Behind a Good-bye there lurks much of the salutation of another beginning—to me, Development, Continuity, Immortality, Transformation, are the chiefest life-meanings of Nature and Humanity . . . .

Why do folks dwell so fondly on the last words, advice, appearance, of the departing? Those last words are not samples of the best . . . . But they are valuable beyond measure to confirm and endorse the . . . faith of the whole preceding life.

Suggested Reading*

WHITMAN'S POETRY AND OTHER WRITINGS:

An American Primer. Rockland, Me.: Bern Porter, 1972.

Autobiographia. Folcroft, Pa.: Folcroft Library Editions, 1973.

Complete Poetry and Selected Prose. Edited by J. E. Miller, Jr. San Jose, Calif.: H. M. Gousha, 1959.

Democratic Vistas and Other Papers. New York: Scholarly Reprints, 1970.

Lafayette in Brooklyn. Folcroft, Pa.: Folcroft Library Editions, 1973.

Leaves of Grass. Ithaca: Cornell University Press, 1961.

Specimen Days. Edited by Alfred Kazin. Illus. Boston: David R. Godine, 1971.

Walt Whitman's Civil War. Edited by Walter Lowenfels. Drawings by Winslow Homer. New York: Alfred A. Knopf, 1961.

BOOKS ABOUT WALT WHITMAN:

Allen, Gay Wilson, *The Solitary Singer: A Critical Biography of Walt Whitman*. New York: New York University Press, 1967.

Barrus, Clara, *Whitman and Burroughs, Comrades*. Port Washington, N.Y.: Kennikat Press, 1931.

Daugherty, James, ed., *Walt Whitman's America*. New York: World Publishing Co., 1964.

Deutsch, Babette, *Walt Whitman: Builder for America*. Illus. by Rafaello Busoni. New York: Julian Messner, 1941.

Hoff, Rhoda, *Four American Poets*. New York: Henry Z. Walck, 1969.

Stoutenburg, Adrien, and Baker, Laura N., *Listen America: A Life of Walt Whitman*. New York: Charles Scribner's Sons, 1969.

* The author has listed popular editions for convenient reference.

Samuel Clemens

Samuel Clemens
/ Meet Mark Twain

Sam Clemens decided that the time had come for journalist to turn author. He would write a book. The raucous days of California mining camps and Dan'l, "The Celebrated Jumping Frog of Calaveras County," now lay behind him. He turned to the East, where he was relatively unknown. Shortly after his arrival in New York City, January 12, 1867, Clemens called at the office of George Carleton, Broadway publisher. Carleton's business methods were not always the best, but they brought results. His editions, often reasonably priced, had wide sales among the general public, and Sam was concerned with profits, not eye appeal. A book printed on pulp paper and bound in paper covers read just as well as one printed on vellum and bound in calfskin, and it could be sold to many more people.

Sam used his resourcefulness to get past the clerk in the reception room. He knew that Carleton was aware of his reputation west of the Mississippi River. And he had at one time submitted a manuscript to Carleton, although without success. He hoped this new approach would be more rewarding than the first. But rebuff again awaiting him. Sam had barely crossed the threshold of Carleton's office when the publisher stormed: "Books—look at those shelves! Every one of them is loaded with books that are waiting for publication. Do I want any more? Excuse me, I don't. Good morning." And the door slammed in Clemens' face.

At that moment the crestfallen author could hardly have looked ahead twenty-one years to a chance meeting with Carleton in Switzerland, when the subdued publisher would confess:

169

"I refused a book of yours and for this I stand without competitor as the prize ass of the nineteenth century."

Sam Clemens grew up in Hannibal, Missouri, on the Mississippi River, though he was born in another town. In his *Autobiography* he recalled:

I was born the 30th of November, 1835, in the almost invisible village of Florida, Monroe County, Missouri. . . . The village contained a hundred people and I increased the population by 1 per cent.

The village had two streets, each a couple of hundred yards long; the rest of the avenues mere lanes, with railfences and cornfields on either side. Both the streets and the lanes were paved with the same material—tough black mud in wet times, deep dust in dry.

Most of the houses were of logs . . . . There was a log church, with a puncheon floor and slab benches. A puncheon floor is made of logs whose upper surfaces have been chipped flat with the adz. The cracks between the logs were not filled; there was no carpet; consequently, if you dropped anything smaller than a peach it was likely to go through. The church was perched upon short sections of logs, which elevated it two or three feet from the ground. Hogs slept under there, and whenever the dogs got after them during services the minister had to wait till the disturbance was over. In winter there was always a refreshing breeze up through the puncheon floor; in summer there were fleas enough for all.

Sam's parents, John and Jane Clemens, came from Tennessee.

"My parents removed to Missouri in the early 'thirties," Clemens wrote. "I do not remember just when, for I was not born then and cared nothing for such things." His father "at last pitched his tent in the little town of Florida . . . . He 'kept store' there several years but had no luck, except that I was born to him."

Sam was the fifth of six children, in a family where there were always financial difficulties. Thirteen-year-old Orion, Sam's brother, assisted his father in the store. Mr. Clemens, a lawyer, was elected justice of the peace and from this post acquired the permanent title "Judge."

The future of Florida was promising when the Clemenses first settled there. Located on the Salt River, fifty miles from the Mississippi, it looked forward to the commerce natural to a river town. But later, when the railroads were extended across the continent, creating a more efficient method of transportation for passengers and freight, Florida slipped into obscurity. Judge Clemens, realizing the town no longer held promise for his future as a businessman and lawyer, moved his family and his store to Hannibal, a new and flourishing town located on the Mississippi River. Manufacturing plants were already being established there, and trade was active. Hannibal ranked itself next in importance to St. Louis as a river town.

The family settled temporarily in the Pavel Hotel while Judge Clemens and Orion set up a store with goods shipped overland from Florida. The Judge also opened a law office to add to his income.

The top society of Hannibal consisted of merchants and professional men, who wore tall hats, ruffled shirtfronts, and swallowtail coats. They lived in pleasant brick or frame houses; some had built mansions with colonnaded entries, after the style of all southern architecture of the period. They owned land and slaves.

It was to this class that Judge Clemens felt he and his family belonged, but there was one thing missing: the means to provide such a life-style. He built a frame house, which he felt was suitable to his standing in the community.

"At first my father owned slaves," Clemens recorded in his *Autobiography*, "but by and by he sold them and hired others by the year from the farmers. For a girl of fifteen he paid twelve dollars a year and gave her two linsey-woolsey frocks and a pair of 'stogy' shoes—cost, a modification of nothing . . . ."

As a boy, Sam began to have vague doubts about the institution of slavery. Although he could not recall ever having seen a slave auction in Hannibal, he wrote in his *Autobiography:* "I vividly remember seeing a dozen black men and women chained to one another, once, and lying in a group on the pavement, awaiting shipment to the Southern slave market. Those were the saddest faces I have ever seen. Chained slaves could not have been a common sight or this picture would not have made so strong and lasting an impression upon me."

The "nigger trader," he added, was loathed by everybody and regarded by Hannibal citizens as a kind of "human devil who bought and conveyed poor helpless creatures to hell." The town folk saw the plantation as "hell; no milder name could describe it."

But Sam and the other children would have been lonely without the protection and company of the Negro slaves. Jennie and Uncle Ned, acquired when finances were good, had total charge over the Clemens children. In the evening, the children gathered around the fireplace while the two slaves entertained them with spine-tingling legends which always began, "Once 'pon a time." Thus Clemens could write in his *Autobiography*: "In my school-boy days I had no aversion to slavery. . . . No one arraigned it in my hearing; the local papers said nothing against it; the local pulpit taught us that God approved it . . . . In Hannibal we seldom saw a slave misused . . . ." Considering this atmosphere of total acceptance of slavery, it was not surprising that even Clemens' mother saw nothing wrong with it. "When slavery perished," Clemens wrote, "my mother had been in daily touch with it for sixty years. Yet, kind-hearted and compassionate as she was, I think she was not conscious that slavery was a bald, grotesque and unwarrantable usurpation."

Sam was sickly as a child. He was scatterbrained, apparently unstable, and showed little potential. He was easily impressed by improbable situations; whatever was weird, fantastic, or considered taboo in more polite circles held an inevitable attraction for him. He had a strange sense of humor which expressed itself in even stranger ways. His favorite way of showing his humor was through pranks, which were designed to startle but never to hurt the person upon whom they were played. Although Sam would not deliberately hurt anyone, there were times when some of his more imaginative pranks backfired and he found himself the object of a spanking from his father. He could not stand to be confined in the house or schoolroom, a punishment which was often the end result of one of his pranks. Such punishment served to drive him to his ultimate refuge, the river— his solace, playground, and real school. When he walked in his sleep, which he often did, he frequently headed toward the river unless he became ensnared in a dark corner of the house where his family would find him huddled in the morning.

Judge Clemens had a difficult time making a living. He had little if any time to spend with his wife and children. He never laughed and was strict in his rule of the home. Amusements which he might have shared with them he considered foolish, a waste of time better used to increase their income. After the family moved to Hannibal, he was even more absorbed in his business affairs. He sent Mrs. Clemens and the children back to Florida every summer, to her brother's farm. On one occasion, the three-year-old Sam was left in Hannibal, to be brought to the farm a few days later by the Judge.

On Sunday morning, the day Sam and his father were to leave, Judge Clemens arose early. He left Sam asleep, intending to wake him when he was ready to leave. But, preoccupied with his usual concern over business affairs, the Judge forgot and left without him. The moment he arrived at the farm and saw Mrs. Clemens' questioning expression, he remembered his son, locked in the empty house alone for many hours and probably crying by now. Without even dismounting from his horse, he quickly rode back to Hannibal, where he found the little boy safe. He was lonely but not terribly distraught because during the interim he had discovered the wonders of an old meal sack in a corner of the storeroom. There was a tiny hole in the sack which Sam's nimble fingers had patiently enlarged, allowing the meal to pour out in an increasingly greater flow and creating a fascinating form of entertainment for him.

Uncle John's farm was a source of delight to Sam and contributed much to his boyhood. "I can remember the bare wooden stairway in my uncle's house," he wrote, "and the turn to the left above the landing, and the rafters and the slanting roof over my bed, and the squares of moonlight on the floor . . . ." He further described moments when he listened to "the raging of the rain on that roof, summer nights, and how pleasant it was to lie and listen to it, and enjoy the white splendor of the lightning and the majestic booming and crashing of the thunder. It was a very satisfactory room . . . ."

Returning with his brothers and sisters to school in Hannibal at summer's end saddened Sam. He had little taste for school, disliked the confinement, and chafed under the rules and regulations imposed on him. But he learned to read and write in spite of himself.

During Sam's early school years the family's perpetual financial difficulties increased, necessitating the sale of their entire household possessions and their slave Jennie. But when Judge Clemens' law practice picked up two years laters, allowing a new household to be established in a new home built on Hill Street, Sam's boyhood ripened into his Tom Sawyer days.

Sam, like his fictional character Tom Sawyer, "was not the Model Boy of the village," but then who would have wanted to be the "Model Boy," with his hair combed and his shoes on all the time? Sam's hair seldom felt a comb, and shoes were only something to keep his feet warm in winter. The model boy would never have played hooky from school; Sam skipped class every chance he got. Being the model boy would have been the most uninteresting existence Sam could imagine. Instead, he was now a strong, healthy nine-year-old, and the last thing he wanted to be was a mother's boy.

The main attraction in Hannibal for Sam was the Mississippi River, the path to all adventure and a gateway to the world: "not a commonplace river, but on the contrary . . . in all ways remarkable," as he described it in *Life on the Mississippi*. There were islands in the river which could be reached by raft or swimming. Sam and his friends sat on the shore and watched the riverboats, "long and sharp and trim and pretty . . . great volumes of the blackest smoke . . . rolling and tumbling out of the chimneys—a husbanded grandeur created with a bit of pitch-pine just before arriving at a town . . . ."

Sometimes Sam and Tom Blankenship, his best friend, "borrowed" a canoe and paddled to one of the islands, where, as described by Huck Finn, "on every old broken-down tree you could see rabbits and snakes and such things; and when the island had been overflowed a day or two they got so tame, on account of being hungry . . . but not the snakes and turtles—they would slide off in the water. The ridge our cavern was in was full of them. We could 'a' had pets enough if we'd wanted them."

Sam spent most of his summer days on the river in some kind of homemade raft or lolling on the shore with a fishing pole in his hand and his eye on the "floating palaces" which daily glided up and down the river. "When I was a boy," he wrote later in *Life on the Mississippi*, "there was but one permanent ambition among my comrades in our village . . . . That was, to be a steamboatman." The possibility of actually taking a trip aboard one of the magnificent steamboats was remote, almost beyond Sam's comprehension. But every man has his breaking point, and Sam had his. One day a river packet stopped at Hannibal to take on passengers and freight. Amidst the excitement and frantic activity which always accompanied the arrival of a steamboat, Sam crept aboard. The crewmen were too rushed and concerned with the loading of freight to notice him, concealed under a lifeboat on the upper deck.

When the signal bells rang, the steamboat moved away from the dock. Sam felt the mounting tension of thrill and fear combined: thrill from actually being aboard one of these floating miracles, and fear of what would happen to him if he should be discovered. He did not have long to wait. While the sun shone above and none of the crew or officers were in sight, he came from his hiding place and reclined on a bale of cotton. The changing scenery was beautiful, delighting his young heart and fulfilling his wildest expectations. But then dark clouds gathered, casting long shadows across the landscape. It began to rain and Sam retreated to the shelter of the lifeboat. But he did not pull his legs in quickly enough, and a crewman who happened to be passing by at that moment caught him by the feet and extracted the kicking, wiggling, protesting Sam from his hiding place. He was put ashore at the next stop and later welcomed home to Hannibal with a spanking from his father.

Most of the incidents recorded in *The Adventures of Tom Sawyer* were based on fact and give a clear picture of Sam's boyhood. Tom Sawyer was a combination of Sam and two of his friends. Sid, Tom's younger brother, was modeled after Sam's little brother Henry. The enviable Huck Finn was inspired by Tom Blankenship, who never took a bath and had no idea what the inside of a schoolhouse looked like.

Sam, like his fictional counterpart Tom Sawyer, was lazy when it came to carrying out constructive activity. No one understood his shiftless nature better than his father. At one time Judge Clemens put Sam to work with a hatchet to remove cracked plaster from the walls of a room. As the work progressed it demanded more than could be accomplished within easy reach from where Sam stood. It did not occur to him to get a chair or ladder on which to stand and chop away the upper sections of the plaster. From Sam's point of view, the logical approach to this part of the work was to lie on his back on the floor and throw the hatchet at the remaining patches of plaster.

When not in school or occupied by some chore of his father's making, Sam was usually at Tom Blankenship's house. Tom and his father lived in an old barn which they had converted into a makeshift house not far from the Clemens home. To Sam, Tom represented all that he ever wanted to be as a boy: independent, free in thought and action, with no one to answer to. Sam was too young to realize that Tom's plight was a sad one, his mother having died some years before and his father being an irresponsible alcoholic. The thing that counted with Sam was Tom's seemingly infinite store of information on such important subjects as hunting, fishing, and trapping and his miscellaneous knowledge of Indian spells, signs, and hoodoos.

Although Sam and Tom were incurable pranksters, they shared one inflexible rule: never abuse an animal. People were different! Sam and Tom were, on occasion, a plague to the peace-loving citizens of Hannibal. Sam seldom went to Sunday school, and Tom never saw the inside of a church building. Their favorite Sunday morning occupation was rolling large boulders down Holliday's Hill to frighten the good folks driving to church in their carriages. But Sam's cat was another matter. His constant companion, it even went with him to Uncle John Quarles' farm every summer, tucked cosily into a basket. The cat, a privileged member of the household, always sat on a chair next to Sam's during the meal hour and was the recipient of tidbits smuggled by its master.

Sam's Tom Sawyer days actually lasted a very short time. Sam was twelve when his father died, in 1847, leaving the family destitute. Sam became a printer's apprentice at a newspaper, thus assuring himself of food, lodging, and clothes, though he later claimed he got "more board than clothes, and not much of either." When his brother Orion started another paper in Hannibal, Sam, now a journeyman printer, joined him in the business.

Sam had been quick to learn the printing trade and became an excellent workman. While still an apprentice, he could run his press in time to whatever popular tune happened to come to mind. In his spare moments, he liked to print popular songs and poems on silk or colorful cotton to present to favorite girl friends.

During this period, Sam continued some sporadic schooling, but his real education was the general knowledge he gained from books, pamphlets, and the newspapers for which he set type. But it was not until he reached the Nevada Territory several years later that he would turn a serious hand to writing. While he was still working for Orion, two articles he wrote were published in *The Saturday Evening Post*, but this spark of talent quickly faded.

After Orion's weekly failed, Sam became a drifter for several years. He worked for a while in the composing room of the *Evening News* in St. Louis, spent a brief period in New York City, and from there went to Philadelphia, then back to New York.

Eventually growing homesick for friends and family in Hannibal, Sam the wanderer returned home, but he stayed for only a short time. A year of restless change had instilled in him a dissatisfaction with the limited horizons of Hannibal. He joined Orion in his new printshop in Keokuk, Iowa, where he remained for eighteen months, then moved on to Cincinnati, and from there to St. Louis.

Sam's vivid imagination had not yet found its proper expression in the creativity of writing but rather took the form of grand schemes to amass a fortune. One of these schemes hinged on a planned trip to the headwaters of the Amazon River in South America, where he expected to find and cultivate cocoa. He was receiving a small income from travel letters he had begun to write for a newspaper in Keokuk. To reach South America he first had to travel to New Orleans. The most convenient means of transportation for such a trip was by steamboat down the Mississippi River.

Sam embarked on the river steamer "Paul Jones" in April, 1857, for the trip to New Orleans. Although he had been wandering across the North American continent for half a decade, it was not until he boarded the "Paul Jones" that he became aware that he "was a traveler." "I became a new being," he later recorded in *Life on the Mississippi*. "When we stopped at villages and wood-yards, I could not help lolling carelessly upon the railings of the boiler-deck to enjoy the envy of the country boys on the bank."

"I soon discovered two things," Clemens recalled in the book. After he reached New Orleans he found "that a vessel would not be likely to sail for the mouth of the Amazon under ten or twelve years; and the other was that the nine or ten dollars still left in my pocket would not suffice for so impossible an exploration . . . even if I could afford to wait for a ship. Therefore it followed that I must contrive a new career."

Unconsciously, Sam had already decided on his "new career": that of a riverboat pilot. He sought out pilot Horace Bixby of the "Paul Jones" and presented his argument. "At the end of three hard days he surrendered," Sam recorded in *Life on the Mississippi*. "He agreed to teach me the Mississippi River from New Orleans to St. Louis for five hundred dollars, payable out of the first wages I should receive after graduating. . . . If I had really known what I was about to require of my faculties, I should not have had the courage to begin."

There was a science to the task of acquiring the knowledge necessary to become, and remain, a riverboat pilot. Twelve hundred miles of the shifting, ever-changing river had to be learned; since tides and currents made constant changes in the channels, each trip presented the challenge of following a new channel route.

"There's only one way to be a pilot," Bixby told Sam, "and that is to get this entire river by heart." A ponderous litter of facts had to be remembered: names of towns, points, bars, islands, bends, and curves. One day Bixby questioned Sam about the shape of Walnut Bend.

"I didn't know it had any particular shape," replied Sam, after some thought.

"My boy, you've got to know the *shape* of the river perfectly," said Bixby. "It is all there is left to steer by on a very dark night. Everything else is blotted out and gone. But mind you, it hasn't the same shape in the night that it has in the daytime."

On another occasion Bixby brought him up sharply with the query: "Didn't I tell you that a man's got to know the river in the night the same as he'd know his own front hall?"

"Well," Sam responded, "I can follow the front hall in the dark if I know it *is* the front hall; but suppose you set me down in the middle of it in the dark and not tell me which hall it is; how am *I* to know?"

"Well," answered Bixby, "you've *got* to, on the river!"

"Two things seemed pretty apparent to me," Clemens recalled in later years. "One was, that in order to be a pilot a man had got to learn more than any one man ought to be allowed to know; and the other was, that he must learn it all over again in a different way every twenty-four hours."

Sam Clemens received his pilot's certificate on April 9, 1859, just two years after he had boarded the "Paul Jones" for his first trip down the Mississippi. His pilot's salary was equal to that of the Vice President of the United States at that time. He was a pilot for four years, and at one period during his career on the river he piloted "The City of Memphis," "the largest boat in the trade and the hardest to pilot." "Consequently," he commented to Orion in a letter, "I can get a reputation on her." He added, with excusable pride, "And the young pilots who used to tell me, patronizingly, that I could never learn the river cannot keep from showing a little of their chagrin at seeing me so far ahead of them. Permit me to 'blow my horn,' for I derive a *living* pleasure from these things . . . ."

Sam had only one accident during his service on the river: he ran aground in a cornfield. But even then no one was hurt, and the boat was not damaged.

Sam was the most fashionably dressed pilot afloat. He always wore blue serge or white duck suits, depending on prevailing weather conditions. His shirts were inevitably striped, and his shoes patent leather. He kept his beard neatly trimmed in muttonchop style and wore his pilot's cap at a jaunty angle. Fellow pilots found him the best of companions because of his extensive knowledge of history, literature, and the sciences, and lady passengers reveled in attention from the dashing young pilot.

Sam, still in his twenties, was now equipped with one very respectable trade, printing, and a highly respected profession, piloting on the Mississippi River. He had never lacked self-confidence, but these added distinctions lent an undeniable luster to the young dandy.

The Civil War ended Sam's career as a pilot. The river was closed to all except military traffic. Sam, whose steamer was fired on by Union troops as a warning to come to a stop, admitted that he was "not very anxious to get up into a glass perch and be shot at by either side." He made his final trip up the Mississippi as a passenger on the "Uncle Sam," the last steamer to make the trip from New Orleans to St. Louis after the outbreak of the Civil War.

Sam left the steamer at Hannibal just in time to join one of the militia companies which had been formed in the town. Missouri itself was in a state of internal conflict. It was a border state and espoused slavery but had chosen to side with the North officially. This decision did not relieve the conflicts between local divisions within the state, nor within the many families who were divided on the war issue—the Clemens family not excepted.

The militia troop to which Sam suddenly found himself attached declared itself allied to the Confederate Army. It made little difference to Sam which side of the cause his troop chose to take, since his heart was really not in the effort. His company, as it turned out, was a motley crew. Sam was second lieutenant, but there was no first lieutenant. Out of fifteen men in the company, there were only three privates, all of whom refused to do picket duty, even when threatened with court-martial.

Sam's field equipment consisted of an extra pair of boots, two blankets, a homemade quilt, a frying pan, a carpetbag, one small valise, his overcoat, twenty yards of rope (which did come in handy), and an umbrella.

When the company moved out from Hannibal, Sam mounted a mule named Paint Brush, and arranged his "military" equipment as best he could. The first night out there were two alerts: one when a row of cornstalks waving in the wind was mistaken for an advancing enemy column, and the other when the one man who agreed to do picket duty shot his own horse, which had slipped its tether and nuzzled him from behind.

The first morning in the field, the cavalry, as it chose to define itself because of a few horses commandeered from Hannibal residents, prepared to advance. Paint Brush refused to pass through a small stream, the first obstacle in the path of march. Another member of the cavalry tied Sam's trusty rope around the mule's neck and pulled it across the stream. According to Sam's account of the incident, he was still on the mule's back. When the soldier turned to observe the progress, he saw that the other end of the rope was under water and that Sam and the mule had disappeared from sight. As the soldier continued to pull on his end of the rope, Sam and the mule emerged from the depths of what was actually a swollen stream.

Sam's military career lasted for two weeks, at the end of which time he traded his Confederate uniform for buckskins and rode west in a stagecoach. His separation from the Army was precipitated by a mishap. One night the cavalry bedded down in the hayloft of a barn. Sam, a man of sound sleeping habits, rolled out of the hayloft in his sleep and landed on the floor below. He sprained his ankle. The injury was not severe enough to incapacitate him, but what little enthusiasm he still had for army life was knocked out of him in the fall. He decided, then and there, to sever his military "connection," which was about to come to an end the next day anyway, since the "leader" of the cavalry had reached a similar decision. The cavalry broke up in the morning, and each man went his own way.

But Sam was not at liberty for long. Lincoln had appointed Orion Clemens to the post of Secretary of the new Territory of Nevada, and Sam went along as his brother's secretary.

"Each of us put on a rough, heavy suit of clothing, woolen army shirt and 'stogy' boots included," wrote Clemens in *Roughing It*, "and into the valise we crowded a few white shirts, some underclothing and such things. My brother, the Secretary, took along about four pounds of United States statutes and six pounds of Unabridged Dictionary; for we did not know—poor innocents—that such things could be bought in San Francisco on one day and received in Carson City the next." Sam "was armed to the teeth with a pitiful little Smith & Wesson's seven-shooter," which he "thought . . . was grand."

Shortly after arriving in the Nevada Territory, he "was smitten with the silver fever." He joined one of the prospecting parties "leaving for the mountains every day, and discovering and taking possession of rich silver-bearing lodes and ledges of quartz. Plainly this was the road to fortune."

The road was paved with glitter, but not from silver or gold. Sam soon discovered his "strike" was nothing more than mica "that isn't worth ten cents an acre."

"So vanished my dream," the author mused in *Roughing It*. "So melted my wealth away. So toppled my airy castle to the earth and left me stricken and forlorn. Moralizing, I observed, then, that 'all that glitters is not gold.' "

While in the mining fields, Sam had begun writing articles for a Keokuk, Iowa, newspaper. Not wanting himself, a future millionaire, to be known as a "camp scribbler," he signed his articles "Josh." During this period he also contributed to the Virginia City *Territorial Enterprise*, and when his "strike" failed, he joined the reporting staff of this publication. The "Josh" letters had appeared in the *Enterprise* and had won for him immediate popularity with staff and readers alike. He thus began his career as a writer on a note of success, which continued to increase throughout his entire career.

When Sam was sent to Carson City to cover the activities of the Nevada legislature for his newspaper, he decided to adopt a pen name. The first report he sent to the *Enterprise* from Carson City, dated February 2, 1863, was signed "Mark Twain." Thereafter, everything he wrote for publication bore this signature. The name caught on like wildfire, and almost immediately friends, members of the legislature, and fellow newspaper reporters began addressing him as "Mark."

Within a few weeks after his work began appearing in California newspapers, the name Mark Twain was as well known on the Pacific coast as it was in the Nevada Territory, even though its origin was remote to both sections of the country. "Mark twain" was a navigational term used on the Mississippi River. It meant "two fathoms deep" and indicated safe water. The leadsman, who took soundings to determine the depth of the water, called out "mark twain" to let the pilot know the channel was deep enough for the riverboat to enter. The river term "mark twain" had echoed through all of young Sam Clemens' dreams about becoming a riverboat pilot.

Sam's Virginia City career ended abruptly, as did all things in his life. While temporary editor of the *Territorial Enterprise*, he became involved in what he considered a humorous verbal war with the editor of the Virginia City *Union*, a rival journal. The dispute concerned a local effort to raise money for the Sanitary Fund, predecessor to the American Red Cross and active for the Union Army during the Civil War. Sam's comments reflected his Confederate sympathies and ignited the anger of the local citizens. Although he sent an apology to those whose indignation he had aroused, which calmed them to a point, that part of the controversy which appeared in print continued at fever pitch. It had become personal, and it seemed to Sam that the only way to end it was to challenge his rival editor to a duel. But the duel never came off. The appearance of this challenge in print violated a new law, which made it a felony to send or accept such a challenge. The fact that Sam's challenge was printed in the *Enterprise* made it impossible for law enforcement authorities to ignore it. Sam, with his close friend and second in the proposed duel, Steve Gillis, left the Nevada Territory for San Francisco.

Sam and Steve, former compositor for the *Enterprise*, arrived in San Francisco in May, 1864. They both found jobs with the San Francisco *Morning Call*, but Sam quickly discovered the strict policies of this newspaper interfered with the rugged, creative individualism with which "Mark Twain" had come to be identified. He soon grew bored with the job because his work as a reporter was routine.

The only exciting part of the day was that devoted to the daily newsletter which he wrote for the *Territorial Enterprise* back in Virginia City. Since he was paid thirty dollars a week for these newsletters, Sam felt secure in giving up his job on the *Morning Call* to spend a few months in and around California's mining camps. This left him free of all responsibilities except the newsletters, into which he could pour impressions of whatever caught his eye as colorful and unique, and mining camps were colorful!

Had it not been for his free-swinging months among the gold miners on Jackass Hill near Tuttletown, California, Sam's first major short story might never have been written. He had had a story, "Those Blasted Children," reprinted in the New York *Sunday Mercury* from the San Francisco *Golden Era*, and two short stories published in the Virginia City *Territorial Enterprise*. But "Jim Smiley and His Jumping Frog" (later known as "The Celebrated Jumping Frog of Calaveras County"), which appeared in the New York *Saturday Press* on November 18, 1865, was his first work ever to have its original publication in the East. It was immediately copied by newspapers and magazines throughout the country, bringing "Mark Twain" into homes in every part of the United States. The realization that he was becoming a nationally known writer began to dawn on Sam Clemens, and he sought more than ever to find new material for his increasingly popular pen.

The Sandwich (Hawaiian) Islands had recently become very important to California's commercial interests. As such, they were a main topic of conversation and appeared in news items and magazine articles throughout the state. Sam reasoned that a new series of articles on these exotic islands would have great appeal to readers, especially in California. Since he was still not employed by any one newspaper, he was free to write the series for the paper that offered the highest price. The editor of the *Sacramento Union* commissioned him to do the series and agreed to pay his expenses.

Although Sam's nature was well suited to the lazy life of the Hawaiian Islands, he was a tireless sightseer. In order to write the articles he had to learn as much as he could about the islands, in what was originally planned as a month-long visit. In his travels through the islands he was surprised to find many friends whom he had made during his varied career as a printer, Mississippi River pilot, and newspaper reporter in the Nevada Territory. The Hawaiian Islands then offered the newest frontier for exploration and exploitation to the ever-restless pioneer.

Sam's most daring adventure in his tour of the islands took place when he and his guide crossed the floor of the active Kilauea Volcano at night. He wrote in *Roughing It:*

After dark half a dozen of us set out, with lanterns and native guides, and climbed down a crazy, thousand-foot pathway in a crevice fractured in the crater wall, and reached the bottom in safety. . . .
. . . the floor looked black and cold; but when we ran out upon it we

found it hot yet . . . it was likewise riven with crevices which revealed the underlying fires gleaming vindictively. A neighboring caldron was threatening to overflow . . . . So the native guides refused to continue . . . everybody deserted except a stranger named Marlette. . . . His pluck gave me backbone. . . . We skipped over the hot floor and over the red crevices with brisk despatch . . . . Then we took things leisurely . . . jumping tolerably wide and probably bottomless chasms . . . threading our way through picturesque lava upheavals . . . . When we got fairly away from the caldrons of boiling fire, we seemed to be in a gloomy desert . . . a suffocatingly dark one . . . .

By and by Marlette shouted 'Stop!' I never stopped quicker in my life.

Sam returned to California three months later instead of the allotted one month, his head and notebooks brimming with fresh ideas. The series of articles he wrote about the islands was so successful that he soon found himself launched on a lecture tour—subject: the Hawaiian Islands.

Sam's next adventure was a commission from the *Alta California*, a daily newspaper, to write a series of articles on a pleasure cruise from America to Europe and the Holy Land. He was not the only newspaper reporter aboard the steamer "Quaker City" when she sailed from New York Bay, but he proved to be the busiest. He wrote almost a quarter of a million words during the voyage; fifty-three travel letters were dispatched to the *Alta*, six to the *New York Tribune*, and three to the *New York Herald*. Not quite two years later, in July, 1869, his book, *The Innocents Abroad*, a humorous and unforgettable account of the cruise, was published.

"For months the great Pleasure Excursion to Europe and the Holy Land was chatted about in the newspapers everywhere in America," Sam reported on the first page of this book. "It was a novelty in the way of excursions—its like had not been thought of before, and it compelled that interest which attractive novelties always command. It was to be a picnic on a gigantic scale."

This cruise eventually brought about a permanent change in

Sam Clemens' life. Among the passengers was the eighteen-year-old Charles L. Langdon, of Elmira, New York, with whom Sam became close friends. One sun-drenched September afternoon, when the ship lay anchored in the Bay of Smyrna, Greece, Sam was visiting in Langdon's cabin and there saw a miniature portrait of his sister Olivia.

Sam did not meet Olivia Langdon, "that wonderful miracle of humanity," until several months after his return from abroad. It was in December, 1867, that Charlie Langdon invited Sam to meet him and his family at the St. Nicholas Hotel in New York City. Sam had been working as a correspondent in Washington, D.C., for several newspapers and came to New York City to spend the holidays. On the evening of December 27, he and the Langdons attended a reading by Charles Dickens. Five days later, on New Year's Day, he called on Livy at the New York City home of a friend with whom she was staying. He arrived at ten in the morning and left thirteen hours later.

Sam did not see "little Miss Livy" again until late August, when he was invited by the Langdons to visit them at their Elmira home. His work as a reporter in Washington, lecturing, and the preparation of *The Innocents Abroad* interfered with his courtship of Livy. But on February 4, 1869, they were formally engaged and were married almost a year later.

They settled in Buffalo, New York, in a commodious home—a gift from Olivia's parents—and Clemens took up duties as part owner and one of the editors of the *Buffalo Express*, a daily newspaper. On November 7, 1870, their first child, a son, was born. He was named Langdon, after Olivia's family.

A few weeks after their marriage, Sam wrote a friend: "If all of one's married days are as happy as these new ones have been to me, I have deliberately fooled away thirty years of my life. If it were to do over again I would marry in early infancy instead of wasting time cutting teeth and breaking crockery."

Sam later wrote in his *Autobiography* that Livy's "character and disposition were of the sort that not only invite worship but command it. . . . She was always cheerful; and she was always able to communicate her cheerfulness to others." Reviewing a portion of their life together many years later, he wrote:

During the nine years that we spent in poverty and debt she was always able to reason me out of my despairs and find a bright side to the clouds and make me see it. In all that time I never knew her to utter a word of regret concerning our altered circumstances, nor did I ever know her children to do the like. For she had taught them and they drew their fortitude from her. The love which she bestowed upon those whom she loved took the form of worship, and in that form it was returned—returned by relatives, friends and the servants of her household.

Clemens' first book, *The Celebrated Jumping Frog of Cala-veras County, and Other Sketches*, published May, 1867, had been a great success; his next book, *The Innocents Abroad*, published a few months before his marriage, was in demand before it reached the bookstalls. He had taken the manuscript west with him, where his literary friend and adviser, Bret Harte, "read all the MS. of the 'Innocents' and told me what passages, paragraphs, and chapters to leave out—and I followed orders strictly." Harte had been to Clemens in San Francisco what William Dean Howells would become on the East Coast: the refiner of his hastily written and overexuberant material.

Clemens had given up his reporting job in Washington before he and Livy were married. He had had his fill of politics and politicians. Besides, he wanted to arrange his affairs more substantially for his new role as husband and head of a household.

"I most cordially hate the lecture field," he had written his mother at this time. But the lecture platform offered the most lucrative returns for his talent, and he proceeded on a new tour. One hundred dollars a night was his average earnings on such a tour, and he often took in more. This income, minus the ten per cent which went to his agent, rapidly accumulated into a substantial bank account.

While Clemens was in Boston making arrangements for his first lecture tour with James Redpath's Boston Lyceum Bureau, he met William Dean Howells, then assistant editor of *The Atlantic Monthly*. Their first encounter was in the office of James T. Fields, located over the Ticknor and Fields Bookstore. Howells had written an extremely complimentary review of *The Innocents Abroad* for *The Atlantic*. Consequently, the first thing Clemens did on his arrival in Boston was to call on Howells. The meeting was very cordial. Later Howells wrote of it:

At the time of our first meeting, which must have been well toward the winter, Clemens (as I must call him instead of Mark Twain, which seemed always somehow to mask him from my personal sense) was wearing a sealskin coat, with the fur out, in the satisfaction of a caprice, or the love of strong effect which he was apt to indulge through life. I do not know what droll comment was in Fields' mind with respect to this garment, but probably he felt that here was an original who was not to be brought to any Bostonian book in the judgment of his vivid qualities. With his crest of dense red hair, and the wide sweep of his flaming mustache, Clemens was not discordantly clothed in that sealskin coat, which afterward, in spite of his own warmth in it, sent the cold chills through me when I once accompanied it down Broadway, and shared the immense publicity it won him.

It was a year before Howells and Clemens met again. Their second meeting took place at a Boston literary luncheon, over "beefsteak with mushrooms." From this time on their friendship became warm. As author and editor, Clemens and Howells shared an exceptionally constructive association. Howells, like Clemens, had grown up on the Mississippi River, a fact that seemed to lend a special flavor to both their literary and personal relationships.

Possibly because of their similar childhood backgrounds,

Howells possessed exceptional insight into Clemens' work, crude though it was in its original stages. It was Howells' literary perception that contributed to the transformation of Clemens from a rough-hewn journalist into a polished writer of humor and satire. The fact that *The Innocents Abroad* had been reviewed by *The Atlantic Monthly* had, in itself, brought to Clemens the realization that he, a western writer, had been recognized by the literary capital of the United States.

Several years after he and Olivia settled in Buffalo, Clemens sold his interest in the *Buffalo Express* and moved to Hartford, Connecticut. Six months before they moved to Hartford, the Clemenses' second child, Suzy, was born, and ten weeks later, Langdon, their son of two years, died. Two daughters, Clara and Jean, were born in Hartford. Only one of Clemens' children, Clara, outlived him.

Hartford, in contrast to Buffalo, was a center of literary activity where many well-known writers made their homes. Clemens knew most of these men and women, among whom were Charles Dudley Warner, editor of the Hartford *Courant* and co-author with Clemens of *The Gilded Age*, and Harriet Beecher Stowe, author of *Uncle Tom's Cabin*. Warner lived next door to the home Clemens built in Hartford, and Mrs. Stowe lived across the street.

The Clemenses' new house was the most elegant in the western section of Hartford at that time. It boasted nineteen rooms and five bathrooms—a relatively new interior feature. There was a billiard room on the third floor, to which Clemens escaped when he needed relaxation from his writing. A porch like the deck of a riverboat ran along one side of the house. The house had Gothic turrets and a balcony on the second story in the shape of a pilot-house. The home was planned with the thought of large and lavish entertainments. During one year of the family's seventeen-year occupancy of it, their living costs ran to one hundred thousand dollars because of these extravagant affairs. Of their generous hospitality, a neighbor, the Reverend Thomas K. Beecher, remarked: "You must know that yours is one of the few restful homes in which intelligence, culture, luxury and company combine to the compounding of a pleasure which every visitor longs to taste again."

The house at Nook Farm, the suburban community in which Clemens had built, cost much more than he had originally planned. But Livy was the daughter of a wealthy family, and it was her husband's avowed intention to give her everything her father would have provided for her. Just the five acres on which the house stood cost thirty-one thousand dollars. Added to that was the seventy-thousand-dollar cost of the house, plus twenty thousand dollars spent to furnish it. These expenses left a large dent in Clemens' bank balance. Added to all these expenditures was the family's rising cost of living. Something had to be done immediately to increase their income, or bankruptcy would soon be upon Sam Clemens. The author had no intention of turning to his wife's wealthy family for financial assistance. There was but one answer: the lecture platform.

Reluctantly, Clemens returned to the lecture circuit he had given up at the time he purchased a share in the *Buffalo Express*. Redpath was now offering him as much as five thousand dollars a week for a series of lectures to be delivered throughout California, but it was all Clemens could do to drag himself away from Livy and the children. His home and family were the center of his affections, and to leave them for a lecture tour on the opposite side of the continent was the last thing he wanted to do.

Clemens' work as a lecturer occupied his winter months. Summers were spent in literary labors at Quarry Farm, near Elmira, New York. The farm belonged to Livy's sister. On a far corner of the property she built a study for her now famous brother-in-law. It was shaped like a pilothouse. He described it in a letter:

It is octagonal, with a peaked roof, each octagon filled with a spacious window, and it sits perched in complete isolation on top of an elevation that commands leagues of valley and city and retreating ranges of distant blue hills. It is a cosy nest, with just room in it for a sofa and a table and three or four chairs . . . .

In another letter he wrote: "On hot days I spread the study wide open, anchor my papers down with brickbats and write in the midst of the hurricanes . . . ."

Clemens made his first trip to England in 1872 and was received with many honors. Later that year, he returned to England with his family, and delivered a series of lectures throughout the British Isles.

Roughing It was published in February, 1872. This book, though reasonably successful, did not live up to the expectations Clemens had for it. It was written under extremely difficult circumstances. Clemens' work on it had been interrupted by a series of deaths among family and friends and a period of critical illness for Livy. There were times during this period when Clemens was convinced that his career as an author was at an end. It was Howells' review of the work in *The Atlantic Monthly* that turned the tide for the book and the author's career. Although *Roughing It* produced only half the income which his earlier book, *The Innocents Abroad*, had brought, it was enough to reassure Clemens about his writing ability and to renew his confidence that he could support a wife and children by his pen.

The financial problems created by Clemens' extravagant living habits were increased by his investments in inventions. He became interested in a typesetting machine, the invention of a Hartford jeweler, and had, by the mid-1880's, poured more than eighty thousand dollars into what turned out to be a failure. He held patents on typewriters, fancy scrapbooks, games, and an envelope-making machine. Once, when he had the chance to invest in Bell's telephone, he declined. "I was the burnt child," he said, "and I resisted all these temptations." In spite of his doubts about the telephone, Clemens was the first resident of Hartford to have one installed in his home. He was also the first American writer to use a telephone in a story.

His own invention, a self-pasting scrapbook, was to him a "great humanizing and civilizing invention." In view of the fact that a type of self-pasting scrapbook is now being marketed, he may have been more premature than mistaken in his judgment of its usefulness, although how "humanizing and civilizing" an effect the invention would have on mankind is debatable. The pages of his scrapbook had columns of an adhesive substance which, when moistened, would hold scrapbook items. The scrapbooks were manufactured in several sizes.

As Clemens' finances became more of a problem, he frantically searched for ways of increasing his income. His book *The Gilded Age*, co-authored with Charles Dudley Warner, was published in 1873. This he turned into a play, "Colonel Sellers," which toured the country and ran for over one thousand performances. The profits—over a hundred thousand dollars—were divided equally with John T. Raymond, the actor who played the leading role. The success of this play gave Clemens the illusion that he was a dramatist, and a few years later he collaborated with Bret Harte on a play titled *Ah Sin*. Even Clemens was forced to admit that the more this play was cut by the director, "the better it got." "I never saw a play that was so much improved by being cut down," he confessed. "I believe it would have been one of the very best plays in the world if his [the director's] strength had held out so that he could cut out the whole of it."

In spite of the rewarding profits from *Roughing It*, *The Gilded Age*, and "Colonel Sellers," Clemens still needed money. The debts incurred by extravagant habits and unwise investments forced him to return yet again to the lecture platform. Livy was even more disturbed by this necessity than Clemens, who loathed even the thought of leaving his comfortable home and warm family circle for the dreary months on tour. Livy, the "delicate little beauty," as she was once described by Howells, wrote Sam: "I do hope this will be the last season that it will be necessary for you to lecture. It is not the way for a husband and wife to live if they can possibly avoid it, is it?"

If they were living beyond their means, she had a solution:

. . . we will either board or live in a small cottage and keep one servant, will live near the horse cars so that I can get along without a horse and carriage—I *can not* and I *will not* think about your being away from me this way every year, it is not half living—if in order to sustain our present mode of living you are obliged to do that, then we will change our mode of living.

But Sam Clemens had no intention of changing his mode of living, and he knew that he could not afford to give up the lecture platform. With his winters taken up in lecture tours, his summers must necessarily continue to be devoted to the production of books. During the summer of 1874, he recalled thoughts that had come to him just four days after his marriage. These were happy memories of his childhood in Hannibal. Now, as he sat in his study at Quarry Farm, he began to translate these memories into fiction. The fictionalized town of Hannibal became "the poor little town of St. Petersburg," and his recollections of his own boyhood became the model for the adventures of a character whom he named Tom Sawyer. Although he was writing some fifty pages of the *Tom Sawyer* manuscript a day, he made no further mention of the story until the following summer, when he described the work as it was beginning to take form:

"Since there is no plot to the thing," he wrote Howells, "it is likely to follow its own drift, and so is as likely to drift into manhood as anywhere—I won't interpose." This was two weeks before he completed the manuscript.

When he wrote again to Howells, he said, "I have finished the story and didn't take the chap beyond boyhood," and later he added, "It is *not* a boy's book, at all. It will only be read by adults. It is only written for adults."

Later, after thinking the matter over, Clemens changed his mind and wrote Howells: "Mrs. Clemens decides with you that the book should issue as a book for boys, pure and simple—and so do I. It is surely the correct idea."

Clemens placed complete reliance on Howells' opinions concerning his work. A word of praise from the editor was all that he needed to confirm his sometimes shaky self-confidence in the work at hand. "Yours is the recognized critical Court of Last Resort," Clemens once wrote to Howells; "from its decision there is no appeal; and so, to have gained this decree of yours before I am forty years old, I regard as a thing to be right down proud of."

"Tom Sawyer is simply a hymn put into prose to give it a worldly air," Clemens commented upon publication of the book in December, 1876. *The Adventures of Tom Sawyer* was an instant success and a classic from the moment of its appearance in print. Its author had originally attempted in 1872 to write the story as a play. As such, it failed. Again, in 1883, he wrote a dramatization of the novel, but it, too, was rejected as a play. Yet as a novel, the story has continued to fulfill Howells' prophecy upon his first reading of the manuscript: "altogether the best boy's story I ever read. It will be an immense success."

On April 11, 1878, the Clemens family embarked on another trip to Europe to gather material for a European travel book Clemens planned to write. After he settled the family in Heidelberg for the summer, he and an assistant left on a walking tour of Germany, which he described in the book *A Tramp Abroad*:

. . . we made the customary trip into the Black Forest. We were on foot most of the time. One cannot describe those noble woods, nor the feeling with which they inspire him. A feature of the feeling, however, is a deep sense of contentment: another feature of it is a buoyant, boyish gladness; and a third and very conspicuous feature of it is one's sense of the remoteness of the work-day world and his entire emancipation from it and its affairs.

It took Clemens fourteen months in Europe to collect the material for *A Tramp Abroad*. While on a trip to Paris he got the idea for another book, *Joan of Arc*, which he wrote several years later when the family was again living in Europe.

After a European stay of almost a year and a half, the Clemens family found their Hartford home sweeter than ever. They had made many new friends during their sixteen months abroad. Many of these people came to the United States and were welcome guests in the Clemens home. Clemens loved his home and family so deeply that he found few reasons sound enough to take him away from them except on business. Everything was in the home that they could possibly need; therefore there was seldom anything to take them out.

Since *Tom Sawyer*'s success had temporarily relieved Clemens of the necessity for extensive lecturing, he was now free to devote most of his time to writing. When he wearied of his work, he could always relax for an hour or so shooting billiards. A few shots at the table in his third-floor billiard room, and he felt refreshed; new ideas began to stir, and he returned to his desk.

Ever since his arrival in New York City in 1866 Clemens had thought "the Mississippi [River] . . . well worth reading about." He was now in need of fresh material for a book, and the Mississippi could, he thought, answer his need. In 1882, accompanied by a stenographer, he boarded "The Gold Dust," a river steamer, at St. Louis for a trip down the river to New Orleans. Since he wanted to keep his identity a secret, he used an assumed name. He had not been on a riverboat since his last nervous trip up the river at the beginning of the Civil War. But the twenty-one-year absence rolled back instantly, and it was not long before the old river pilot gave in to his greatest yearning: He paid a visit to the pilothouse.

The Mississippi River and its pilots had not changed so much that Sam Clemens was not recognized by the pilot of the "Gold Dust," who had been observing Clemens' effort to sight old landmarks from the lower deck. Although the pilot did not reveal Clemens' identity, he soon tricked him into taking the wheel. Clemens later admitted feeling a little unsure at first, but he quickly began to recognize the old landmarks which had not seemed visible before he took over the wheel.

When the pilot again took over the wheel, he confessed to Clemens that he had recognized him as having been the senior pilot who, many years earlier, had examined him for his license. Clemens did not remember the occasion.

Clemens spent much of the remainder of this trip, which was his last down the Mississippi, in the pilothouse, and even stood night watch. He wrote Bixby, his old instructor, "I'd rather be a pilot than anything else I've ever done in my life."

In 1881, Clemens had taken over publication of his own books, publishing *Life on the Mississippi* in 1883. His publisher had died, and although he had paid for the publication of several of his own books, he had not before been the actual publisher. He named his new firm Charles L. Webster and Company, after his nephew, who managed it. By 1884 he was publishing the works of other authors as well as his own. The first of his own works to come off his presses after *Life on the Mississippi* was *The Adventures of Huckleberry Finn*, in 1885. *Huckleberry Finn* is a sequel to *Tom Sawyer*. Unlike many sequels, which are often inferior works when compared with the original story from which they grew, *Huckleberry Finn* is an excellent story and stands entirely on its own as a novel. It has a much greater appeal for adult readers than does *Tom Sawyer*. Many knowledgeable people in the field of American literature feel that

Mark Twain is more likely to be remembered for *Huckleberry Finn* than for *Tom Sawyer* or even for *Life on the Mississippi.*

Clemens' publishing firm prospered. After the success of the publication of *Life on the Mississippi* and *The Adventures of Huckleberry Finn*, he reissued his earlier books, which were to travel to every corner of the country with "broken-down clergymen, maiden ladies, grass widows and college students," to share a place of respect on parlor tables along with Shakespeare and the Bible.

A few months after the appearance of *Huckleberry Finn*, Webster and Company published Ulysses S. Grant's two-volume *Personal Memoirs*. Grant, after having served two terms as President of the United States, had lost his life savings through investments offered him by a dishonest stockbroker. In an effort to help him recoup his lost fortune, or at least a portion of it, Clemens gave him seventy per cent of all the profits from the elegantly-bound edition. Before Grant had even finished writing the manuscript, Webster and Company had arranged for over one hundred thousand advance sales of it. Grant was suffering from his final illness during the preparation of the manuscript. Clemens, who had the deepest admiration for the former President and General, described his unwavering determination to complete the work before his death in order that his wife might receive the profits from it:

So he sent for a stenographer, and dictated 9,000 words at a single sitting!—never pausing, never hesitating for a word, never repeating—and in the written-out copy he made hardly a correction. He dictated again, every two or three days—the intervals were intervals of exhaustion and slow recuperation—and at last he was able to tell me that he had written more matter than could be got into the book. I then enlarged the book—had to. Then he lost his voice. He was not quite done yet, however:—there was no end of little plums and spices to be stuck in, here and there; and this work he patiently continued, a few lines a day, with pad and pencil, till far into July, at Mt. McGregor. One day he put his pencil aside, and said he was done —there was nothing more to do. If I had been there I could have foretold the shock that struck the world three days later.

The *Memoirs* paid Grant's widow about half a million dollars in royalties, as Clemens had predicted it would. But its publication forced Clemens' company beyond the sum allocated for the project. Although the book sold well, and was actually the most successful achievement in Clemens' publishing venture, it marked the beginning of the end of his firm. In an attempt to expand the annual list of publications and thereby increase revenue, Clemens directed the firm's manager to solicit autobiographies, memoirs, and biographies of famous personalities. At best, this was not a substantial approach to operating a publishing house. Proposed projects began to fail; many never got beyond the planning stage. By 1888, Clemens' private journal reflected the approaching crisis:

Sherman (Life of) proves to be unprofitable. Demand a reconstruction of contract placing power in my hands where it belongs. Refused? Go into court. Second: Demand dissolution. Go into court. Can I be held for debts made beyond the capital? I will buy or sell out.

Since the spring of 1886, the thing has gone straight down hill, towards sure destruction. It must be brought to an end, February 1, at all hazards. This is final.

After the publication of *Huckleberry Finn* Clemens was so involved in business affairs that he did not produce any new work until the publication of *A Connecticut Yankee at King Arthur's Court* in 1889. *A Connecticut Yankee* grew out of research he had been doing for many years on another book, *Joan of Arc*, which would not be published until 1895. *A Connecticut Yankee*, from which two moving pictures have been made, was not well received in England because Clemens used it as a vehicle to criticize certain English laws and traditions which he considered outmoded and limiting to individual development.

Clemens' financial problems continued to increase. His investment in the Paige Typesetter became a greater burden each year, with no promise of return, and his living expenses continued to soar. Since living expenses were lower in Europe, Clemens reasoned that the practical thing to do would be to move his family abroad until he could work out a permanent solution to his financial problems. The thought of leaving his home in Hartford was heartbreaking, but he felt there was no other choice. He reassured himself with the thought that the baths in Europe would be beneficial to Suzy, ailing for several years, and the change of climate good for Livy, who also suffered an illness. But he confessed to Howells: "Travel has no longer any charm for me. I have seen all the foreign countries I want to see except heaven and hell."

Clemens knew, in the secret chambers of his heart, that they would never return to the home they had loved so well and in which they had been so happy. As he walked through the empty rooms, shortly before their departure, he could not help recalling the seventeen active years spent there, with the perennial flow of guests, entertainments, daily joys, and sorrows. Now the walls were bare, the windows draped with sheeting, the furniture, carpets, and books packed into a warehouse. As he left the house, Sam Clemens slowly and thoughtfully pulled the front door closed and turned the key in the lock with a deliberate, final gesture. Yesterday was gone. Tomorrow, June 6, 1891, they would sail for Europe to remain, except for a brief visit to Quarry Farm in 1895, until 1900.

Once on board the ship bound for France, Clemens made a brief though significant entry in his journal: "Tom and Huck die."

The Clemens family spent the next nine years restlessly shifting from one place to another: France, Germany, Italy, Switzerland, Austria, England, Sweden, and back to Italy. Much of this movement was brought on by the need for money, and Clemens was always popular as a lecturer. He charmed and was charmed by many of the crowned heads of Europe who sought him out. Upon receiving a dinner invitation from William II, Emperor of Germany, his daughter Jean remarked, "Papa, the way things are going, pretty soon there won't be anybody left for you to get acquainted with but God." Carmen Sylva, Queen of Rumania, wrote him, "I owe you days and days of forgetfulness of self, and troubles, and the intensest of all joys—hero-worship!"

Before he left the United States, Clemens had completed work on the manuscript of *The American Claimant*, the first book he had written after several years of silence. He syndicated it for twelve thousand dollars, a relatively small sum in the face of his past spending habits. Temporarily, however, his financial difficulties were relieved. He also contracted for a series of six travel letters to be written from abroad, for which he was to be paid one thousand dollars each. For several years after going abroad to live, Clemens traveled back and forth across the Atlantic every few months in an effort to nurse his failing investments back to a sound state of health. Eventually, he lost everything; all he had left to support his family was his voice, with which to lecture, and his pen, with which to write for publication.

Even the royalties from his published works vanished when the economic depression of 1893 struck the United States. It was time for Sam Clemens to settle down to serious work again to help rejuvenate some of his lost finances. He moved his family to the Villa Viviana, near Florence, Italy, and began the task of completing *Joan of Arc*, which he had begun several years earlier in Berlin. The old villa fitted the mood of the book on which he was at work, its atmosphere so inspirational that Clemens completed two other books as well, both of which he had been writing on and off for several years: *Tom Sawyer Abroad* and *Pud'n' Head Wilson*. He also wrote the short story, "The Million Pound

Bank Note," while at the Villa. He had been working on *Joan of Arc* for fourteen years; twelve were spent in research and preparation, and two in writing. All of Clemens' books took years to produce and were usually written spasmodically until he either decided to finish a work or was forced by a pressing need for cash to complete it. It was only then that he settled down to concentrated and uninterrupted literary labor, which could span a year or more. This did not include the many months he often spent in revising a manuscript, a disagreeable though unavoidable part of his authorship.

When the Clemenses returned to America and Quarry Farm in 1895, it was for a brief time only—a stop on what was to be a globe-encircling lecture tour. Jean and Suzy, now young women, remained at the farm, while Livy and Clara accompanied Clemens on tour. They left Elmira, New York, by train on July 14 for the West Coast. From there, they traveled westward, over continent and ocean. Clemens described this trip in *Following the Equator*:

It was warm work, all the way, and the last fortnight of it was suffocatingly smoky, for in Oregon and British Columbia the forest fires were raging. We had an added week of smoke at the seaboard, where we were obliged to wait awhile for our ship. . . . We sailed at last; and so ended a snail-paced march across the continent, which had lasted forty days.

Clemens opened his lecture tour in Cleveland, Ohio, and moved westward at a slow pace, delivering lectures and readings of his works in such cities as Duluth, Minneapolis, St. Paul, Butte, and Winnipeg and Vancouver in Canada. At Vancouver he sent a bank draft of five thousand dollars to New York City to be placed against his debts, the reason for this extensive tour. Although he had been reluctant to leave the comforts of home, Clemens reveled in the crowded auditoriums, the ovations, and the generous hospitality that greeted him and his family at every point along the route. Success did not go to waste on Sam Clemens; he relished every glorious moment of it.

From Vancouver, the Clemenses embarked for Hawaii and continued their tour through New Zealand and Australia, finally reaching Bombay, India. "A bewitching place, a bewildering place, an enchanting place—the Arabian Nights come again!" Clemens found in India all that his friend Kipling had promised. In *Following the Equator* he wrote:

> ... the land of dreams and romance, of fabulous wealth and fabulous poverty, of splendor and rags, of palaces and hovels, of famine and pestilence, of genii and giants and Aladdin lamps, of tigers and elephants, the cobra and the jungle, the country of a hundred nations and a hundred tongues, of a thousand religions and two million gods, cradle of the human race, birthplace of human speech, mother of history, grandmother of legend, great-grandmother of tradition, whose yesterdays bear date with the moldering antiquities of the rest of the nations . . . .

Clemens' lecture tour ended in London, where he and his family settled in a house in Chelsea for the winter of 1896. They kept their presence in London a carefully guarded secret because the author needed a period of uninterrupted quiet in which to complete *Following the Equator*. If his friends in London had known of his arrival in the city, he would have been so deluged with invitations and visitors that work on the manuscript would have come to a complete halt.

While visiting Vienna in 1899, Clemens wrote to Howells: "I have been reading the morning paper. I do it every morning—well knowing that I shall find in it the usual depravities and basenesses and hypocrisies and cruelties that make up civilization, and cause me to put in the rest of the day pleading for the damnation of the human race. I cannot seem to get my prayers answered, yet I do not despair."

The biting satire expressed in these lines reflects Sam Clemens' growing bitterness toward life. In later years, disillusionment was the keynote in his business and personal affairs. Suzy died in 1895; Jean and Livy were ill, and both would die before him. He lost and squandered several fortunes in publishing and hare-brained investment schemes and no longer owned even his home, until he built Stormfield in Redding, Connecticut, two years before he died. Frugality, defensiveness, conservatism, limits, self-inquiry, inwardness—all unnatural to him—seemed forced upon him. His expansiveness appeared crushed by this untoward burden, and his work began to define this attitude of self-doubt and despair. He wrote articles and books, among them *What Is Man?* attacking established standards of religion and undermining what little faith Livy found in the orthodox creeds to which she turned after Suzy's death.

Just one year before his death, Clemens remarked to Albert Bigelow Paine, his foremost biographer, "I came in with Halley's comet in 1835. It is coming again next year, and I expect to go out with it. It will be the greatest disappointment of my life if I don't go with Halley's comet."

Sam Clemens was not disappointed. He died April 21, 1910. But Mark Twain lives on forever.

Suggested Reading*

MARK TWAIN'S NOVELS AND OTHER WRITINGS:

Adventures of Huckleberry Finn, The. New York: Airmont Publishing Co., 1967.

Adventures of Tom Sawyer, The. New York: Platt & Munk, 1960.

Autobiography of Mark Twain, The. Edited by Charles Neider. Illus. New York: Harper & Row, 1959.

Celebrated Jumping Frog of Calaveras County, The. New York: Dover Publications, 1971.

Clemens of the Call: Mark Twain in San Francisco. Edited by Edgar M. Branch. Illus. Berkeley, Calif.: University of California Press, 1969.

Complete Essays of Mark Twain. Edited by Charles Neider. New York: Doubleday & Co., 1963.

Complete Humorous Sketches and Tales of Mark Twain. Edited by Charles Neider. New York: Doubleday & Co., 1961.

Complete Short Stories of Mark Twain. Edited by Charles Neider. New York: Doubleday & Co., 1957.

Connecticut Yankee in King Arthur's Court, A. New York: AMSCO School Publications, 1970.

Life on the Mississippi. New York: AMSCO School Publications, 1969.

Prince and the Pauper, The. New York: Scholastic Book Services, 1972.

BOOKS ABOUT MARK TWAIN AND HIS FAMILY:

Allen, Jerry. *The Adventures of Mark Twain*. Magnolia, Mass.: Peter Smith.†

Clemens, Clara. *My Father, Mark Twain*. Illus. Reprint. New York: AMS Press.†

Eaton, Jeanette. *America's Own Mark Twain*. New York: William Morrow & Co., 1958.

Kaplan, Justin. *Mr. Clemens and Mr. Twain: A Biography*. New York: Simon and Schuster, 1966.

McNeer, May, and Ward, Lynd. *America's Mark Twain*. Boston: Houghton Mifflin Co., 1962.

* The author has listed popular editions for convenient reference.
† Publication date not listed.

Meltzer, Milton. *Mark Twain Himself: A Pictorial Biography.* New York: Bonanza Books, a division of Crown Publishers, 1960.

Miers, Earl S. *Mark Twain on the Mississippi.* New York: World Publishing Co., 1957.

Proudfit, Isabel. *River Boy: Mark Twain.* New York: Julian Messner, 1940.

Stoutenburg, Adrien, and Baker, Laura Nelson. *Dear, Dear, Livy: The Story of Mark Twain's Wife.* New York: Charles Scribner's Sons, 1963.